The Operator's Blueprint

10 Core Values to Build Culture, Drive Profit, and Scale High-Performance Teams

Tim Murphy

ISBN: 979-8-9958340-0-7 (hardcover)
ISBN: 979-8-9958340-1-4 (paperback)
ISBN: 979-8-9958340-2-1 (ebook)

To the Boomers team I had the privilege to lead and learn alongside—through real work, real challenges, and shared accountability, we tested and refined the principles reflected in this book.

Though our paths diverged after the sale, the lessons learned together endure in these ten core values and represent a lifetime of leadership learning.

Contents

Foreword

When you spend your career in the attractions and hospitality industry, you quickly learn that great operations are about more than rides, food, or entertainment. They are about people—leaders who set the tone, teams who deliver the experience, and cultures that guide how decisions are made every day.

Over the years, I've had the opportunity to work alongside many leaders in this industry who understand that truth. Tim Murphy is one of those leaders.

Tim's career has spanned a wide range of operational environments, but one theme has consistently stood out in his leadership approach: the belief that culture drives performance. Organizations that clearly define their values—and then hold themselves accountable to them—create stronger teams, better guest experiences, and more sustainable businesses.

The Operator's Blueprint captures many of those lessons. In this book, Tim shares practical insights from decades of leadership experience and translates them into a framework that operators can apply inside their own organizations. The ideas presented here are not theoretical. They come from real operational environments where leadership, culture, and accountability directly impact results.

For leaders responsible for building and scaling organizations, the principles outlined in this book offer a thoughtful guide for aligning teams, strengthening culture, and driving performance.

The attractions and hospitality industries continue to evolve, but one thing remains constant: Organizations succeed when their leaders are intentional about the culture they build.

That is the message at the heart of *The Operator's Blueprint.*

—Ken Whiting
President, Whiting's Foods
Former Chairman of the Board, International Association of
Amusement Parks and Attractions (IAAPA)

Introduction
Why These Ten Core Values—and Why Now

Don't hide your scars. They make you who you are.

—Frank Sinatra

Most businesses don't fail because they're based on a bad concept. They fail because the foundation of the company is weak. This has been a common theme throughout my career as a CEO and turnaround specialist. When I took over at Boomers Parks in the summer of 2020, for instance, the company was failing for a number of reasons. Yes, the pandemic hit revenues hard, but profits had already been sliding for months. That wasn't the only issue. Staff were disengaged. Managers weren't trained to analyze financial reports. The rides were outdated. The bathrooms were dirty. Online reviews were brutal. I managed to turn Boomers around before moving on four years later, but not with a singular fix. The entire company needed to go through a series of fundamental changes that quickly transformed it from the inside out. Those changes were rooted in the ten core values I share in this book— and if your business is struggling, they can work for you too.

Leaders of failing companies often want a silver bullet. They want a straightforward, easy solution to the multifaceted problem they face. I wish it were that simple. In reality, a business is an interconnected system that can only be saved through a holistic approach. Addressing low-hanging fruit like raising prices or hiring new staff isn't enough; you must evaluate the individual parts of your company and get them all working optimally. The purpose of this book is to give you a blueprint designed to improve every aspect of your company simultaneously. That blueprint consists of the following ten core values:

1. **Integrity**: Doing the Right Thing Even When It Hurts
2. **Accountability**: Owning Outcomes, Not Excuses
3. **Safety**: The Promise You Must Never Break
4. **Service**: Making People Feel Seen
5. **Communication**: Clarity Builds Trust
6. **Commitment**: Staying the Course When It Gets Hard
7. **Innovation**: Finding a Better Way
8. **Profitability**: The Engine That Sustains Everything
9. **Partnership**: Winning With, Not Against, Others
10. **Social Responsibility**: Leaving Things Better Than You Found Them

This list is not a set of theories I learned from textbooks. They are the same core values I've used to rebuild struggling organizations—from theme parks to restaurants to family entertainment centers—and turn them into high-performing, profitable, purpose-driven powerhouses. They've worked in companies with thousands of team members and in family-owned businesses with just a handful. They've worked in boardrooms, in crisis situations, and even in my own home.

These core values are not "nice-to-haves." They are nonnegotiables. They form the foundation for a winning culture and a sustainable business model. They can be applied whether you're leading a Fortune 500 company, managing a small department, or guiding your family through life's challenges.

And here's the truth: It's not enough to *know* them. You have to *live* them. Every day. In every decision. Through every challenge. That's when transformation happens.

Why These Values Work Anywhere

Some people hear "core values" and think they're just words on a wall. I've walked into companies with mission statements framed in beautiful glass . . . and a culture completely opposite to the words displayed. Values that live in a picture frame don't move the needle. Values that live in people's actions do.

Whether you're applying these principles to a business, a department, or your own household, the pattern is the same:

- They build trust (**integrity**).

- They create ownership (**accountability**).

- They minimize risk (**safety**).

- They deliver excellence to the people you serve (**service**).

- They ensure clarity (**communication**).

- They drive perseverance (**commitment**).

- They keep you relevant (**innovation**).

- They provide financial direction (**profitability**).

- They expand your reach (**partnership**).

- They give your work meaning beyond profit (**social responsibility**).

The real magic is their interconnectivity. You can't have **innovation** without **commitment**. You can't have **partnership** without **communication**. You can't have **accountability** without **integrity**. Apply them together, and they create a momentum that is almost impossible to stop.

How I Learned These Values

I was raised by Albert Bork Murphy and Jean Griffin Murphy in a noisy New Jersey household with three much older brothers, Steve, Rick, and Harry. This made me the baby of the family and the default tackling dummy, dishwasher, ball-retriever, and reluctant comedian. We were loud, competitive, and always moving. Dad ran multiple businesses—fencing, construction, welding, building homes, and running a miniature golf course and arcade restaurant called the Spirit of '76.

If you lived under Dad's roof, you worked. He had us building fences and homes, doing estimates, shingling roofs, and handing out golf clubs. We served ice cream, slushies, hamburgers, hot dogs, cheesesteaks, and candy at the Spirit of '76. We built masonry chimneys, welded, stacked lumber, and cut pickets for the fence company. Additionally, we took on normal household chores like mowing lawns, shoveling snow, and getting firewood for our two fireplaces and woodstove to heat the house in the winter. Dad would say, "If you're not tired at the end of the day, you didn't work hard enough." I built the work ethic I have today thanks to his example, and there's not a day I don't thank him for it as he rests in heaven with my mother.

Growing up with three brothers nine to fifteen years older meant I rarely won at swimming, basketball, football, or even backyard chores. I learned to compete and cooperate. They also gave me a nickname: "Tard," supposedly tied to the custard stand at the Spirit of '76. For brotherly love, I tolerated it, but I never liked it. It taught me early how words land and why respect matters, even when the intent is "affectionate."

By the time I was sixteen, we had moved from Cape May, New Jersey, to Kissimmee, Florida, near Walt Disney World. I left Dad's businesses to work at EPCOT Center, which opened in October of 1982. My first role was in food service at the Renaissance-style food tent between the United Kingdom and France areas of the park. I wore brown pants, purple boots, a cream-colored blouse, and a rope belt. Today, there's a waterway there leading to the Dolphin, Swan, BoardWalk, Beach, and Yacht Club hotels. Disney is truly amazing—so many changes have taken place since October 1982, and it keeps on growing.

From there, I rotated through the Sunrise Terrace, Stargate, and Odyssey restaurants, then into Cash Control, emptying all the EPCOT and Ticket Center safes at 4 a.m., and later into the Lake Buena Vista hotel arcades and the Fort Wilderness Resort & Campground arcades. I saw some strange things at that campground between 5 and 6 a.m. (usually involving guests running from their tents to the showers in the buff). Eventually, I moved into finance, preparing monthly resort financial statements for the Contemporary, Polynesian, and Disney Inn, known today as Shades of Green. I also consolidated monthly financial statements with the Magic Kingdom and EPCOT to send to Burbank, CA, and handled job costing for the Grand Floridian and Caribbean Beach resorts before they opened. EPCOT in those early days meant thousands of guests every day. It could be chaos, but those are some of my fondest memories. One funny (and not so funny) memory happened at Sunrise Terrace in West CommuniCore, when I spilled hot grease while rushing to keep up with demand. Running twelve fryers at once, I slipped, fell, and burned my arms. The white spots are still there as a reminder.

Those years at home and Disney forged the ten core values that drive this book. They weren't dreamed up in a boardroom; they were lived— on jobsites, behind counters, in cash rooms at 4 a.m., and later in turnaround board meetings under pressure. From the noisy Spirit of '76 to the cash rooms of EPCOT, from fryer burns at Sunrise Terrace to boardroom showdowns at Boomers and the other 150 brands with 10,000 locations I've worked at in my career, these values shaped me. They gave me a framework not only for turning businesses around but for building them to last.

The title of this book—*The Operator's Blueprint*—reflects the architectural nature of the ten core values. They form a deliberate operating design that underpins scalability and performance. I provide a deep dive into each value, demonstrating how you can implement them into your business, team, and life. If my journey proves anything, it's that values aren't theoretical. They're practical tools. When you live them consistently and without compromise, they create not just profit but purpose.

The Self-Assessment Survey

Each chapter concludes with a Self-Assessment Survey that consists of ten questions with a possible total score of 10–50. These diagnostics are designed to translate the book from inspiration into execution. They convert values into observable behavior and measurable operating reality.

A few important notes about these surveys:

- They're not personality tests. They measure what is actually happening in your organization: the behaviors you reward, tolerate, and reinforce.

- Your first score is just your starting point, not your identity. The purpose is clarity, not guilt.

- Scores matter, but holistic patterns matter more. A single low area can undermine several strong ones.

- If you want honest answers, create psychological safety within your team before distributing these tools. Otherwise, you'll get "best possible answers," not truth.

This work starts with honesty. Before you can strengthen your foundation, you have to be willing to examine it as it is, not as you hope it is or wish it were. That's why the journey begins with **integrity**. Everything else depends on it. If you're ready to stop looking for silver bullets and start building something that lasts, turn the page.

1. Integrity
Doing the Right Thing Even When It Hurts

Trust, but verify.

—Ronald Reagan

During my first conversation with a former business partner, he joked, "Some people love me when they see me coming down the street. Others turn away." I understood what he meant at the time and do even more clearly now. He was willing to take advantage of anyone in any way he could when it suited him. The man had enemies.

Hearing that should have been a red enough flag to keep me from partnering with the guy, but I was desperate during a long dry spell between consulting gigs. I needed money to put food on the table for my family, and credit cards were only going to get me so far. I had to get past that hurdle somehow, and this guy had what seemed like a huge number of promising connections. We agreed to go into business together, a move that would go on to hurt me financially in ways that weren't easy to resolve.

At a certain point, this partner stopped putting money into our company. Every challenge we hit fell on my shoulders and became my problem to handle. Many of the promising connections I met weren't operating aboveboard and were apparently known for their shady business tactics. They would come to my partner to sponge off the profits I was working hard to earn for us. I soon came to realize I was being used, and a familiar, sickening feeling grew inside me—one I had first felt early in life and seen in the eyes of my father.

When I was a kid growing up in New Jersey, my parents owned multiple companies. Dad was always busy with fencing, welding, construction, building homes, and their miniature golf arcade restaurant called the Spirit of '76 after the United States Bicentennial. I would help him out, working alongside him and learning from his example. The main lesson from early on was "Always do your best." He was a good entrepreneur but somehow always struggled financially in spite of that fact, and I often wondered why. As I got older, I came to understand the root of the problem: He was simply too gracious. Dad wanted to get along with everyone he met, which for him meant lending money to people who never paid him back. Even friends and family members took advantage of him.

As a teenager, I modeled Dad's generosity and soon began to find myself in situations where I was the one being taken advantage of. I joined the Boy Scouts at a young age, where I started learning about the concept of core values like integrity. After becoming an Eagle Scout at age fifteen, I wanted to help other kids in the program rise to higher ranks but was often pressured into shouldering the weight of their responsibilities for them. They would copy my work or have me do all the planning for our camping trips, taking equal credit for the great results we enjoyed. Over and over, people came into my life, noticed my dedication, and tried to sponge what they could off my efforts. Decades later, as my business partner and his shady connections dragged me into financial ruin, I felt the same inner storm of anger and shame that always comes with exploitation. My rock-bottom moment had come at last.

How had I, with the sincerity and work ethic I'd developed as an Eagle Scout, found myself associated with such people? How had I attracted all that negativity into my life? I didn't want to be working with snakes. Getting used by people who lacked integrity had repeatedly been an obstacle between me and the life I wanted to be living. The same vulnerability that had caused my father to struggle was destroying my career. History on repeat. I knew that in order to change my trajectory, I had to get serious about evaluating the people around me to discern whether they were trustworthy or full of BS. I had to trust but verify. I wanted to operate from a place of honesty like I had as a Scout and work exclusively with others who did too. Integrity became nonnegotiable to me, and maintaining that boundary became my biggest priority.

Ultimately, though my credit took a hit, I was able to dig myself out of that hole by taking on more responsibility at higher-paying jobs. The effects of that experience followed me for years, however. Before taking over the role of CEO at Boomers Parks, the private equity firm funding the company conducted background checks and learned of the financial problems my previous partnership had created for me. They believed in me enough to give me the job anyway, and I always tried to outperform their expectations with gratitude. In that role, I trusted and empowered those I worked with but was always sure to verify that they were doing the things they had said they would do. I would physically visit each park to make sure improvements had taken place. I also analyzed our marketing efforts and financial reports to check that our strategy as a team was working. That was my job.

Every day, we see examples of dishonest people who seem to get away with shady behavior, but those folks all hit a wall eventually. They burn bridges with great colleagues, get terminated from their positions, end up owing millions in debt, or even serve time in prison for stealing. The bottom line in both business and life is that you'll never make real progress with people who lack integrity, the quality of being honest and adhering to strong moral principles with unwavering dedication. This is the first and most important core value in this book. As a leader in business, you've got to be able to trust that your team will do the right thing at all times, even when no one is looking. Without honesty and transparency, distrust will grow and spread through every aspect of your business. Integrity isn't something that can be faked or performed without substance; it's a personal ethos that indicates trustworthiness. It has to be real for true change to take place, and it has to start with you.

What Integrity Looks Like in Business

At the Spirit of '76 when I was a kid, integrity looked like small choices—giving the full scoop of ice cream, not a hollowed-out one; cutting a straight fence line even when it meant re-digging posts; telling a guest, "We messed up. Let's fix it." Disney sharpened all that. In finance, I learned the weight of a number. A rounding "shortcut" could snowball into someone's job on the other end. When those monthly resort statements left Orlando for Burbank, they had to tell the truth, not the story we wished were true. Nobody stood over my shoulder. Integrity meant caring when no one was watching.

Years later, when I stepped into a company whose profit and loss statement looked like a downhill ski slope, there was pressure to "frame" the numbers for investors—push a few expenses, pull some accruals, make the quarter look brighter than it felt. I refused and presented the real picture: ugly in places, fixable with discipline, and honest to the penny. The room around me went silent. Then, over time, something better than applause came: trust. Integrity cost my company a few easy headlines, but it bought us credibility that carried through its turnaround.

In a perfect world where everyone had integrity, how would your business run? Fundamentally, you would know that everyone involved— cashiers, managers, and COOs included—could be trusted to do the right thing at all times, even in your absence. You'd be able to count on them to make responsible choices whether or not someone was watching them. They would know you had their back as a leader and would have yours in return. This mutual trust would allow you to focus on your tasks without having to constantly keep an eye on everyone. You would rest assured that once you had set your expectations and provided adequate guidance, your team would do what it could to meet those standards.

Clearly, we don't live in a perfect world where this dynamic is the norm, but it is possible to form a team where most of its members act from a place of integrity. This forms a foundation of trust at work that helps people feel comfortable addressing challenges together. Your team, especially your managers, will be able to come to you in both good times and bad rather than hiding problems when they arise. You'll be able to feel confident that if and when something goes wrong, you'll be told about it directly. You won't be blindsided by problems without explanations that seem to appear out of nowhere. Small issues will be nipped in the bud early on rather than being avoided and allowed to spiral out of control.

Integrity is the soil from which accountability grows. When your team operates with honesty and transparency, they'll be willing to take responsibility for the specific role they fulfill at your business. With that sense of ownership, they will care about what happens at your company and how its day-to-day operations unfold. When mistakes happen, they will be able to take accountability, apologize if necessary, and make an effort to ensure the same thing doesn't happen again.

Businesses that value integrity are more likely to be consistently profitable in the long run. I've seen this throughout my career while working at companies like Applebee's and Walt Disney World. When no one is stealing, cutting corners, or manipulating the numbers behind the scenes, financial discrepancies are less likely to arise. You won't have to spend as much time investigating gaps between where your numbers are and where they should be.

What Happens When Integrity Is Lacking

In looking for people to hire, look for three qualities: integrity, intelligence, and energy. And if they don't have the first, the other two will kill you.

—Warren Buffett

Without a strong foundation of honesty and transparency, your business will eventually fall apart. It's that important.

One of the biggest threats we all face while entangled with dishonest people is the possibility of getting in hot water with the law. I once worked as a controller, meaning I was responsible for overseeing all accounting-related activities at the company where I was employed. At one point, the owner came to me wanting to alter the numbers on our financial statements because he was going through a divorce. Lying about his income and pretending the company wasn't as profitable as it was would have enabled him to keep more of his money. Immediately, I pictured myself on a witness stand in court, having to testify under oath that I hadn't cooked the guy's books. That wasn't a risk I was willing to take, so I quit the job in the name of self-preservation. Ask yourself, "Am I willing to go to prison for another person's lies?" It shouldn't even be a question, but these are the stakes when integrity is absent at a company.

Another huge threat to your business is dishonesty around problems that arise. Your employees, especially managers, need to be able to come to you and report what's happening, even when they've got news you won't like hearing. I once had an employee carelessly try to jump over a fence. He fell, broke his elbow, and filed a workers' comp claim. It was a dumb mistake that cost our company money, but I was glad no one tried to hide it from me. Hearing about recklessness and unsafe behavior gave me a chance to look at the root of the issue so we could do better. I was able to provide more training and explanation in the area of safety. If the VP who informed me of the workers' comp claim hadn't done so, I wouldn't have had the opportunity to prevent similar carelessness from happening in the future. Dishonesty is *expensive*.

When integrity is lacking within your team, you're also likely to end up working with people who are willing to cut corners or steal from you. This usually manifests in the form of financial discrepancies. I once turned around a theme park where one particular location had mechanics selling go-kart parts out the back door and then ordering new parts on the company's dime at a rate that greatly exceeded that of every other location. It took time and money to figure out why they were spending so much more on parts, but I was eventually able to identify the problem, and the people responsible magically moved elsewhere on their own, as they saw that they were not following the core values of the company. I stuck with integrity, and they realized they did not have it.

Another sign of a lack of integrity is confusion over what the expectations are at your company. When this is genuine, it often stems from a lack of transparency on your part. Employees can't own their part in how a company operates unless they understand the big picture. They need to know how their actions affect the rest of the business. If you're not continually setting clear expectations and explaining how everything works, people won't understand the reasoning behind your policies and why they matter. Transparency from you and your managers is absolutely key.

The primary attitude you'll find in team members who lack integrity is apathy. They don't care about what happens to the company or buy into its values, which quickly leads to problems for everyone. These are people who don't listen during explanations or change harmful behavior after being reprimanded. Instead, they do the bare minimum and hope you won't notice. It's essential to fill your business with employees who are good at what they do and come to the table with the best of intentions.

Implementing Integrity as a Core Value

The temptation to lie or avoid discomfort in order to protect ourselves is universal. You will always encounter people who are willing to be dishonest to get ahead or keep their job. Once you know and accept this, you can create a system in your business that builds trust between you and your team while weeding out bad actors. Following these tips can help you instate integrity as your company's status quo.

Give people the benefit of the doubt at first.

Trust is only real when it's mutual, which means we leaders must extend trust to our team if we're to earn theirs in return. Even people with the best of intentions can fail to meet company standards when they're unclear on what's expected of them. Many can't grasp how important a policy is until they understand *why* it exists in the first place. Start implementing integrity at your company with the assumption that most people on your team want to do their best, even if you're not sure that's the case. Explain with friendliness and clarity what's expected and why. Make the impression that you're a safe and approachable person to talk to. Getting everyone on the same page in a respectful way can go far in helping people improve apathetic attitudes.

It takes time to get to know everyone at your company at a level that reveals their true colors. To turn a business around properly, you have to meet everyone currently employed there, whether they're working in operations, marketing, or food and beverage. Many will be nervous around you initially, knowing you're there to make big changes, and you'll need to see how they function over the course of a few weeks to get a sense of their intentions.

Teach your team, especially your managers, how the numbers work.

A good number of business leaders find financial statements intimidating. They feel math isn't their strong suit and avoid looking at the numbers as much as possible, even when doing so is a key part of their job. That's not integrity. They may also make false or unfair assumptions about the trustworthiness of their superiors, broadcasting the belief that people in the C-suite are spending frivolously from the comfort of their ivory tower while everyone else pinches pennies. By showing them the numbers and teaching them how your company's finances work, you'll be able to empower them to do the best job possible while earning their buy-in.

While I worked as the CFO of Applebee's, I offered bonuses of 10 percent to managers of locations that exceeded financial targets. When they fell short, I met with those managers to explain all the ways they could make the shift from red to black. There were cuts they could make in the areas of landscaping, office supplies, food portions, and more, all of which empowered them to meet their bottom line. Many businesses I've turned around had managers who were simply never taught how to analyze financial statements, but doing so made it clear that we at headquarters weren't asking them to meet impossible targets. Each manager had personal power to move the needle and earn their bonus.

As someone with an MBA in finance, I've analyzed thousands of financial statements and can easily pinpoint the potential source of financial discrepancies, but most managers don't share my background. They aren't trying to fudge the numbers or game the system; they just don't know how to respond in order to solve the problem. When I worked as the CFO at Sonny's BBQ, for instance, certain locations were in the red because the cooks in the kitchen were serving guests outsized portions. We had just bought bigger plates, and the employees were feeling bad that they didn't look full. Their intentions were pure, but those little boosts in portion size were adding up over time. Opening their eyes to how those oversized portions were hurting their profit margins made everyone buy in and follow our guidelines with greater integrity. Transparency was the missing link that turned everything around.

Investigate problems when the cause is unclear.

While some members of your team simply lack information rather than transparency, you will encounter employees with bad intentions who truly can't be trusted. It can be difficult to discern between the two, so it's important to investigate problems rather than firing or reprimanding an employee prematurely. When something goes awry, and you can't put your finger on what's causing the issue, ask intelligent questions. Do your team members know what's expected of them and why? Have you adequately empowered your managers to act like business owners at their locations? What steps have they taken to improve the situation? What's keeping them from hitting their goals? By listening carefully to their answers, you'll eventually be able to discern whether someone is being dishonest with you. Do they listen when you try to help them or respond in ways that tell you they don't care? People with integrity can be trained to improve. Those who don't care about the company or aren't willing to be honest with you cannot.

Go to locations where problems arise.

If you're working a C-suite role at headquarters, it can be tempting to solve problems from the comfort of your office. You might feel like it's enough to analyze reports, send emails, and communicate with managers over the phone. However, you're likely to miss crucial information and make uninformed judgments if this avoidance becomes a habit. Employees can hide dishonesty and problematic behavior far more easily from afar. By going to them at their location to verify they're being honest with you, you'll be able to assess whether they're giving you the full story.

I once took over a company run by executives who hadn't visited their parks in over two years. They were there to collect their checks rather than to solve problems, and the company had gone bankrupt as a result. The CEO and COO both assured me they already had all the information they needed about their company on their iPads. I was critical of this and drove out to the nearest park to verify what was happening on the ground. There, I found numerous telltale signs of overspending and waste that validated the uneasy feeling I had in my gut. Had I remained at the office trying to understand the company's problems from behind the comfort of a screen, we would never have been able to identify the source of those problems and turn the business around.

Fire people you can't trust.

Once you've made a reasonable effort to investigate the source of a problem within your team, you'll be able to make judgments about whether or not you can trust the people involved. To maintain integrity at your company, you have to be willing to fire employees you can't trust as soon as possible. People who lack integrity behave in unpredictable ways. They may be willing to undermine your efforts or go behind your back to avoid accountability. This kind of behavior can fester and become a cancer to the business. When you're reasonably confident someone is dishonest due to patterns in their behavior, it's time to let them go.

When contemplating firing someone, you may worry whether you've gathered enough information to dismiss them without the threat of legal repercussions. There's a real possibility you could get hit with lawsuits related to wrongful termination at some point, but this shouldn't stop you from taking appropriate action to protect your business. Once you've done your due diligence, you'll have more than a gut feeling to go on while justifying your decisions. You'll have financial reports, real-world observations, answers to your questions, and other clarifying information to support your intuition.

Former Secretary of State Colin Powell used to say that when making decisions, he aimed to gather no less than 40 percent and no more than 70 percent of the information he needed. He believed that attempting to exceed that 70-percent mark could cause him to miss the opportunity to act quickly. He called this the "40–70 rule." Experience has shown me the value of this advice. Aiming for perfection will prevent you from moving forward, and this paralysis will kill your business in the long run. Mistakes will occasionally be made, but you can usually course-correct when they occur. Don't allow fear to keep you from cutting dishonest people from your team.

Firing people who lack integrity doesn't have to be personal. It's not your job to criticize others or make judgments about the overall quality of their character. Whether or not they're honest in their personal life is not your concern. What matters is how they operate when they show up to work. Are they going to help you turn the business around, or will they be a hindrance? That's the main issue at the end of the day.

Leading your turnaround efforts with a focus on integrity will enable you to improve every other aspect of the business. With systems in place to weed out dishonest people, you'll be able to instill and strengthen this core value in the members of your team who share the same goals.

I mentioned before that integrity is the soil from which accountability grows. This brings us to our second core value. Next, we'll explore the role accountability plays in helping a business run smoothly.

Key Takeaways

1. **Integrity is the nonnegotiable foundation of any successful business.**

   - Without honesty and transparency, trust erodes, accountability disappears, and problems multiply.

   - A leader's role is to *trust but verify*—extend trust while ensuring commitments are met.

   - Surround yourself only with people who consistently do the right thing, even when no one is watching.

2. **Leaders must actively build systems that foster integrity.**

   - Clearly communicate expectations and *why* they matter to eliminate confusion or apathy.

   - Teach team members—especially managers—how the numbers work so they can own results and operate transparently.

   - Investigate issues directly and in person when necessary to separate misinformation from fact.

3. **Quickly and decisively remove those who cannot be trusted.**

   - Dishonest individuals can sabotage morale, create legal and financial risks, and drain resources.

   - Follow due diligence, but don't let fear of perfection or lawsuits paralyze you; act within the "40–70 rule" to protect the business.

   - Firing for lack of integrity is about safeguarding the company's health, not passing judgment on someone's personal life.

Integrity Self-Assessment Survey

Rate each question from 1 to 5.

(1 = Not true at all / 5 = Consistently true)

1. Do leaders communicate the truth even when results are disappointing?

   Rating: _______

2. Do financial and operational reports accurately reflect reality without manipulation or selective framing?

   Rating: _______

3. Are problems surfaced early rather than delayed until they become crises?

   Rating: _______

4. Do employees feel safe reporting bad news without fear of retaliation or ridicule?

   Rating: _______

5. Are expectations, policies, and standards clearly defined and documented rather than implied?

   Rating: _______

6. When mistakes happen, are they acknowledged and owned rather than minimized or blamed on others?

   Rating: _______

7. Do leaders regularly verify what is happening on the ground rather than relying solely on reports?

   Rating: _______

8. Are policies and standards applied consistently across roles, tenures, and relationships?

   Rating: _______

9. When trust is broken, is it addressed directly and promptly rather than avoided?

    Rating: _______

10. Do people see clear alignment between leadership words, leadership decisions, and leadership behavior?

    Rating: _______

Scoring & Interpretation

- **40–50 (Strong):** Integrity is a cultural norm. Trust is high and reinforced daily.

- **25–39 (Mixed):** Integrity is inconsistent. Truth may depend on personalities, pressure, or politics. Risk is present.

- **10–24 (At Risk):** Integrity gaps are undermining trust and damaging performance. Immediate leadership action is required.

Leader Reflection (Answer honestly!)

1. Where have I delayed truth because it was inconvenient or politically difficult?

2. What standards am I enforcing strictly—and where am I allowing exceptions?

3. Do people believe I want the truth, or do they feel pressure to protect me from it?

4. When was the last time I personally verified reality rather than trusting secondhand reporting?

5. What behavior am I tolerating today that will become tomorrow's culture?

How to Use This Survey

- **Start at the top.** Have the executive team complete it first; integrity failures rarely begin on the front line.

- **Compare perception gaps.** Run it with managers and frontline leaders and look for disconnects. (Leadership often scores higher than reality.)

- **Treat results as behavioral evidence.** Do not debate intent; identify specific behaviors that must change.

- **Use it after "trust moments."** Rerun after incidents, investigations, major misses, audit findings, or leadership transitions.

- **Define two nonnegotiables.** Select one or two integrity behaviors to reinforce immediately (e.g., "bad news within twenty-four hours," "numbers with evidence").

2. Accountability
Owning Outcomes, Not Excuses

Responsibility equals accountability equals ownership.
And a sense of ownership is the most powerful weapon a team or
organization can have.

—Pat Summitt

A handful of years ago, I turned around a failing theme park chain with several locations across California. After taking over, I visited each park to get a sense of what was fueling the company's financial problems. A number of glaring issues were apparent, the most obvious being the distracted, apathetic behavior of the staff. Some of them hung around nonchalantly scrolling on their phones rather than engaging with guests. Few acknowledged my presence or said hello as I walked around. I even found one of the managers playing cards with a couple of employees at a picnic table during his shift. The lack of accountability was palpable to anyone visiting. The team simply didn't care, and it showed.

In chapter one, we discussed integrity, the quality of being honest and having firm moral principles. Accountability, our second core value, describes a person's willingness to accept responsibility for their choices and behavior. In this book, we're talking specifically about responsibility for the tasks in their job description and their ability to meet the expectations of the company. These first two core values are closely related: When a team's members have integrity, they care enough about their jobs to hold themselves accountable at work. That accountability is the fuel that keeps businesses running smoothly, boosting profits over time. Anyone unwilling to take accountability for the position they signed up for is an existential threat to your company.

What Accountability Looks Like in Business

At home, if I left tools in the yard, I found them frozen under ice or snow. Accountability had a way of finding you. At EPCOT, accountability looked like reconciled safes at 6 a.m. If a deposit didn't match the expected totals on our financial statements, you didn't go home. I learned to double count, to write cleanly, to ask for a second set of eyes when something was off. "It's close" wasn't close enough; the numbers had to be exact. When I later arrived at Boomers, the managers there weren't closing on time, food costs were drifting, and seasonal labor "estimates" felt like fiction. We implemented daily huddles, clear opening and closing checklists, and real-time dashboards. The first weeks were rough. People grumbled. A few left. A few were terminated. But the ones who stayed began to take pride in the numbers they owned. We didn't "hope" revenue would appear; we set targets and measured progress. Accountability turned a ship pointed at the rocks into one that could steer.

When all members of a team take accountability for their role, a business can run exactly as it's designed to. Employees can be trusted to stay on task at all times, even when no one is watching. They take ownership of their work as if the company belonged to them personally, aiming for outcomes and impact that reflect their highest potential. They understand what's expected of them and do their best to meet brand standards, representing the business in ways that provide guests with positive experiences. These qualities are key to generating positive reviews online, which in turn brings in more foot traffic and boosts sales.

Typically, people who do a good job of taking accountability at work share a common trait: conscientiousness. They're habitually mindful of what they should be doing and anticipating the next steps they need to take to keep things running smoothly. They pay attention to what's happening around them rather than zoning out on distractions. They're also open to learning new knowledge and skills. Growth comes naturally to team members under these circumstances because they're always looking for ways to improve or become more efficient.

Accountable people also show up on time to meetings, shifts, and events. Employees who habitually show up late or skip important gatherings end up wasting everyone's time. They can also miss important updates and end up making mistakes that impact the whole team. Even with online meetings, accountable people hop on calls a couple of minutes early to ensure everyone can get started on time. During meetings, they pay attention, ask questions, and remain engaged with the task in front of them. These are all ways to show and build collective respect.

Another aspect of accountability is paying close attention to the company's finances. When managers, bookkeepers, and other members of a team take responsibility for the numbers, especially when discrepancies arise, the business stays profitable. They go through all financial statements and review every expense. When crunch time arrives, and more help is needed, like during summers or holidays, they create room in the budget to hire and train additional staff. Mystery problems aren't allowed to compound into massive losses over time. And when they can't solve a serious issue themselves, accountable managers relay it to corporate rather than hiding the problem and hoping it will magically work itself out somehow.

Managers and people in other leadership positions are tasked with more responsibility than those they manage. They must balance the ability to hold the team together with holding them accountable. Even with great staff, no company can run perfectly all the time. Life events happen, people have bad days, customers can be challenging, and mistakes can occur frequently. When conflict arises, great leaders remind employees of their responsibilities in ways that are firm but fair. They take the time to properly explain how things should be done and communicate expectations not once but continually. And when an employee needs to be written up or dismissed altogether, great leaders do the tough work of respectful confrontation because they know it's necessary in the long run. They operate with the best interests of the team in mind, handling uncomfortable problems head-on rather than avoiding them.

What Happens When Accountability Is Lacking

When members of a team aren't willing or able to take accountability for their responsibilities at work, a business can't function as it's meant to. The consequences of this can range from annoyance or inconvenience to bankruptcy or even death, depending on the situation.

Safety, which we'll discuss in more depth in the next chapter, is an area in which accountability is absolutely necessary. You may have employees operating heavy machinery, climbing tall ladders, or working as lifeguards at water parks, for example. If mistakes are made due to negligence on their part, someone could get seriously hurt or even killed. There's no wiggle room here; these team members *must* pay attention and be as cautious as possible during their shift.

A lack of accountability at a business can also raise operation and maintenance costs in the long run. You may, for instance, have vegetation growing in certain areas that needs occasional pruning, broken tiles in bathrooms, or burned-out bulbs in your lighting system. Fixing these problems after they've gotten out of control can be far more hazardous and expensive than dealing with them early. Teams that take accountability for regular maintenance tasks are likely to become more profitable.

With proper accountability, managers and supervisors serve as effective liaisons between the corporate office and employees at the company's various locations. When this doesn't happen, information from headquarters doesn't end up reaching the rest of the staff. Policy updates aren't communicated clearly. Staff members know little to nothing about the company's values or the overall challenges it faces. Meanwhile, those working at headquarters may be in the dark about what customers and staff are experiencing at company locations. Managers who aren't willing to take responsibility for how things are unfolding at their location may end up hiding certain information from their superiors or failing to act at crucial times. Without accountable managers, everything falls apart.

An employee who struggles with accountability is likely to behave dismissively or disconnect at moments when they need to pay attention. They may be unaware of what's expected of them or act as if they're not responsible for certain parts of their job description. You may also have employees who genuinely want to do their best but aren't quite nailing the role they're meant to fulfill. Some people get anxious about asking questions for fear of looking stupid or making a bad impression. The thorough implementation of this core value can go a long way in helping employees who struggle with these issues improve.

Implementing Accountability as a Core Value

Accountability is expressed through responsible words and actions. Implementing accountability as a core value throughout your company involves both modeling what's expected and getting your team to care enough to emulate that behavior. They must be taught how to take responsibility for every aspect of their specific role. Here are some tips for getting them on board:

Model accountability in your own role.

Set the example you want to see. The last thing you ever want to have to say is "Do as I say, not as I do." Be on time, if not early, to all shifts, meetings, and events. Show commitment and enthusiasm, even when times are tough. Apologize directly when mistakes are made. Be attentive, present, and mindful while you're "on." When you say you'll do something, always do your best to follow through. By modeling accountability, you'll give your team an inspiring example to copy in their own role.

Set clear expectations and explain why they matter.

For employees to take accountability, they need a crystal clear sense of what their responsibilities are. You have to explain what's expected of them from the moment they're hired and periodically after they've been trained. Some of this information will apply to everyone in the company, while some will be specific to their role. A crucial step in setting expectations is to explain *why* things must be done a certain way. If employees get the sense that the rules are arbitrary, they may get frustrated or flippant when they're corrected: "What's the big deal? What does it matter?" You'll be a lot more likely to get their buy-in once they know the reasoning behind a policy. For instance, you may have a freezer system at a restaurant that needs to stay at a certain temperature. That temperature needs to be checked daily to ensure the freezer is running properly and keeping food cold enough. The employee responsible for checking the temperature needs to understand food could be wasted if the freezer malfunctions and they fail to check the temperature, resulting in losses for the company. Knowing the stakes will help them remember and follow through.

I've found stories can be an effective way to convey the stakes while explaining certain policies. People remember anecdotes more than anything. They don't want to run into avoidable consequences others have experienced in the past. Every rule exists for a reason. You may have someone in a kitchen cutting food recklessly and tell them, "Hey, these knives are so sharp they can cut through bone. That happened last year to one of the guys who worked here." It doesn't all have to be doom and gloom, of course. You can bring in positive stories about inspirational figures who handled accountability in memorable ways that led to success. I find quotes like the following one can work well too:

The way to get started is to quit talking and begin doing.

—Walt Disney

You can check a team member's understanding of a policy by asking them to demonstrate or role-play it for you. After explaining how to handle a customer complaint, for example, role-play the angry customer and have the employee act out how to handle the situation in real time. Have your chefs show you their cutting skills and how they handle sharp knives. Have your lifeguards pretend they're saving a drowning guest. Have your bartenders practice upselling food items in addition to drinks. Have your delivery drivers pretend they've dropped off a product shipment at an incorrect address. Role-play gives them an opportunity to practice getting through challenging situations in a low-stakes setting where it's safe to have their guard down, which will help them feel more confident when real problems arise. It also gives you an opportunity to provide nuanced feedback in whichever areas they may be struggling. You'll be able to confirm they've understood your expectations and know how to move forward independently. Give your team chances to role-play various situations they may encounter before they start their shifts.

Train your team to anticipate what needs to happen next.

Taking accountability for our role at work involves anticipating what's around the corner so we can be ready to act. On weekends, employees at family entertainment centers can expect to be busy and must be ready to handle crowds. A manager giving a presentation at headquarters can expect their audience to have certain questions and must come prepared with answers. An owner of a theme park can expect to upgrade and replace equipment every so often and must set aside funding for it in their annual budget. It's possible to see all these things ahead of time and create the conditions necessary to deal with them smoothly.

Anticipating what will come next is predicated on the understanding that no one can rest on their laurels at work. No one is ever "done." There's no finish line to cross. Even when your business is profitable and operating as it should, there's always more to learn and creative ways to improve upon what's there. The team must be on the lookout for ways to make the business the best it can be in ways big and small. Even anticipating the needs of a single guest can result in a lifelong customer who sings the company's praises. Attentive service goes a long way.

Give consistent feedback.

Employees need consistent feedback to take full responsibility for their role. Often, mistakes happen and tasks are neglected because people aren't corrected while they're being trained. Set the expectation for employees to be learning new knowledge and skills during their tenure at the company. Let them know they'll be receiving feedback consistently so they can always be learning and leveling up. Most people crave specific feedback—especially positive feedback—so they can know where they stand. Let them know what they're doing well on a regular basis and what they can do to improve when necessary. If you provide frequent praise and encouragement, they'll be more responsive when you share how they can do better. This is a great way to keep lines of communication open and flowing within a team.

Some middle managers run on the mistaken assumption that if an issue is brought up once, it's taken care of. This is hardly ever the case. More likely, they will have to explain a problem or policy multiple times to employees they supervise. They must also follow up with their own superiors about the role they play in reporting expenses and ensuring the business is profitable. Touch base with them to make sure they're taking accountability for their role by communicating effectively with their contacts at work so everyone can be on the same page.

Encourage employees to ask questions.

No one wants to look foolish in front of their peers, especially at work, where poor impressions can harm one's career. This fear keeps a lot of well-intentioned employees from asking questions when they're confused or lacking information. This is especially prevalent at businesses that hire young people working their first job. They may be intimidated by their lack of experience and anxious about taking action without prior approval. You can create a safe environment by assuring employees that there's no such thing as a stupid question. Make it clear that you expect and welcome questions and requests for clarification. Accountable employees stay engaged and make sure they've got all the details in order. A team that never asks questions is likely mentally disengaged or afraid of potential ridicule. Model asking questions often and invite employees to do the same.

Put systems in place to track accountability.

Having formal systems designed to keep employees on track makes it much easier for everyone to remember, prioritize, and carry out their responsibilities. Your team will have certain tasks to carry out based on their role, the shift they're working, and the needs of the business at the time. Create well-written, accessible manuals employees can read while learning to do their job. Provide them with checklists in different areas and have them check items off daily once they've been taken care of. Hold weekly or even daily meetings to get everyone on the same page about expectations. Reward employees who do an especially good job and provide opportunities to improve for those who aren't operating up to par. That might include cocreating a performance plan with that employee or giving a written warning in which potential future consequences are outlined explicitly. Having formal systems in place around accountability helps everyone keep their mind on what they should be doing and how they can improve.

Promote employees who take accountability.

Employees who consistently perform to company standards are the ones you should start talking to about opportunities for advancement. If they manage their job responsibilities to the best of their ability, becoming more efficient month after month, that's a sign they can handle a higher position. Annual risk assessments on each employee or manager should revolve around questions related to accountability. "Can I trust this person to go above and beyond? Do they take responsibility for what they say they'll do?" That's what separates average employees from exceptional ones.

Accountability is the main key to career growth. This single core value can set anyone up for a more successful future. Responsible people are offered more opportunities and end up wealthier in the long run. They're always improving and keeping their mind on what's next for them and those they care about.

We touched on the importance of safety in this chapter, but it's a crucial core value on its own. Next, we'll talk about how values around safety can elevate a business or bring it crashing down.

Key Takeaways

1. **Accountability drives ownership and performance.**

   - Employees who take full responsibility for their roles act like owners, stay on task without supervision, and consistently meet or exceed standards.

   - Conscientious, accountable team members anticipate needs, solve problems early, and directly contribute to profitability and guest satisfaction.

   - Accountability in leadership means addressing problems promptly, setting expectations continually, and confronting underperformance with fairness but firmness.

2. **Lack of accountability is costly and dangerous.**

   - Neglecting responsibilities can lead to higher operating costs, communication breakdowns, safety hazards, and even legal or financial disaster.

   - Managers who avoid responsibility weaken the link between corporate and frontline staff, causing policy failures and eroding company culture.

   - Disengaged employees often hide mistakes, avoid ownership, or fail to act when it matters most—threatening both revenue and reputation.

3. **Leaders must build a culture and system for accountability.**

   - Model the behavior you expect: Be punctual, follow through, admit mistakes, and stay engaged.

   - Set clear expectations, explain the "why" behind policies, provide ongoing training, give consistent feedback, and encourage questions.

   - Use tools like checklists, manuals, meetings, and performance plans to track accountability—and promote those who consistently deliver.

Accountability Self-Assessment Survey

Rate each question from 1 to 5.

(1 = Not true at all / 5 = Consistently true)

1. Are roles and responsibilities clearly defined so people know what they need to own?

   Rating: _______

2. Are commitments followed through on without repeated reminders from leadership?

   Rating: _______

3. When outcomes fall short, do people take ownership instead of deflecting blame?

   Rating: _______

4. Are performance expectations reviewed regularly rather than only when something goes wrong?

   Rating: _______

5. Are missed standards addressed promptly instead of being tolerated for convenience?

   Rating: _______

6. Do leaders hold difficult conversations quickly rather than avoiding conflict?

   Rating: _______

7. Are metrics reviewed, understood, and owned at the level where action can occur?

   Rating: _______

8. Are consequences applied fairly and consistently, regardless of title or tenure?

   Rating: _______

9. Is accountability treated as a cultural expectation, not as an occasional enforcement tool?

    Rating: _______

10. Are people who demonstrate high ownership recognized and developed?

    Rating: _______

Scoring & Interpretation

- **40–50 (Strong):** Ownership is a norm. Execution is consistent, and standards hold under pressure.

- **25–39 (Mixed):** Accountability varies by manager or department; inconsistency creates friction.

- **10–24 (At Risk):** Execution is unstable. Tolerated underperformance is eroding morale and results.

Leader Reflection (Answer honestly!)

1. Where am I tolerating underperformance because addressing it feels inconvenient?

2. Do we hold people accountable to commitments or only to effort?

3. Are expectations truly clear, or do I assume people "should know"?

4. Where have I failed to follow up, allowing standards to drift?

5. Do consequences consistently match behavior?

How to Use This Survey

- **Run quarterly with managers.** Accountability drifts over time, especially with turnover or growth.

- **Tie it to real commitments.** Use current goals, initiatives, and KPIs as the context for scoring.

- **Identify the "tolerance zone."** Pinpoint where low standards are being accepted and why.

- **Create a follow-through system.** Scores should translate into cadence: check-ins, scoreboards, and closed-loop commitments.

- **Coach the middle.** Accountability lives or dies with managers; support them with scripts, training, and reinforcement.

3. Safety
The Promise You Must Never Break

An ounce of prevention is worth a pound of cure.

—Benjamin Franklin

When I was six, I went to a 4-H fair in New Jersey with my family. We were riding a Ferris wheel lined with long neon lights when, on a downturn, one of the lights above us started breaking. Then another broke, and another. Shattered glass fell onto us from above, nicking our skin, as panic ensued. The staff quickly stopped the ride, ushered everyone off, and shut it down for the night. It was an unsettling experience no one ever wants to have when they come to a theme park. We've all seen news reports about people getting stuck on roller coasters and enduring other horror stories on malfunctioning rides. When something like that happens to you as a guest, trust is broken immediately. You wonder what other hazards might be waiting around the rest of the park. This creates bad memories and leads to consequences for the business, like reduced ticket sales, bad reviews, higher insurance costs, or worse. To avoid incidents like these, companies must embrace safety as a core value, creating a lasting impression that guests will have a great experience.

Creating a safe environment is a company's number one job. No one, whether it's a guest or a team member, should ever be or feel unsafe at your business. This isn't just about avoiding accidents or complying with safety regulations. It's also about keeping your business sanitized, clean, and comfortable. You want to create an ambience that's pleasing to the senses and enables people to escape from their problems for a while. Fun, comfortable, hazard-free experiences leave guests with good memories that keep them coming back. Without safety as a core value, no business can succeed for long.

What Safety Looks Like in Business

The white marks I have on my arms aren't just scars; they're reminders. I was moving too fast at Sunrise Terrace at Disney one day, and the kitchen floor, already slick, turned into a skating rink. Safety is often invisible when it's working; you only feel it when it fails. Disney taught the discipline behind the scenes: dry floors, set temps, guarded edges, clear signage. Not to make life harder, but so guests could relax. In family entertainment, speed sells—faster karts, quicker cycles, more throughput. But faster breaks things if you're not disciplined. At Boomers, we shut down tracks to fix issues, pulled equipment from the floor that didn't pass checks, and changed our standard operating procedures even when it meant losing a Saturday's revenue. An injured guest or team member is never worth a great day's sales. Our promise: Families can trust us. No compromise.

A business that's safe, clean, and comfortable is likely to attract repeat guests. When people find a fun place to unwind, forget about their problems, and make great memories, they usually want to come back. Teams with strong values around safety work to create seamless, stress-free experiences that allow guests to relax and enjoy themselves. This results in great reviews, both online and through word of mouth, boosting foot traffic and profits over time.

For teams that achieve this effect, safety is constantly top of mind. They aren't put through safety training once and left to forget what they learned. Instead, they're updated on safety matters frequently through meetings and ongoing training programs. They're trained to follow current CPR and active-shooter drill procedures. They know where the first aid kits, fire extinguishers, and AED devices are stored. They know every escape route on location and work to keep fire exits unobstructed.

They know keeping everyone safe, including themselves, is their number one priority at all times, and they keep an eye out for potential hazards. When they spot dangerous conditions, they immediately act to deal with the problem themselves or alert someone who can. Zoning out is not an option.

Safety-oriented teams also make cleanliness and sanitation part of their regular routine at work. When there's a mess to deal with, they notice and clean it up. They empty trash cans, mop up spills, and straighten out folds in rugs that guests could potentially trip over. They ensure bathrooms look and smell nice and are stocked with soap and hand sanitizer for guests. They disinfect kitchens and other areas where food is being prepared or served. They also wear gloves and follow safety procedures related to preparing food and using sharp objects like knives. Once they've completed a task related to safety or cleanliness, they check off that item on their daily list or find another means of reporting their progress so others can rest assured they've covered their bases. Everyone works together to keep this standard high.

Managers who hold safety as a core value understand their crucial role in keeping guests and employees out of harm's way. Installing and maintaining safety equipment is a regular part of their job. They build nets under trampolines, replace worn belts on go-karts, and level out uneven concrete. They put up fences and signage to guide guests away from areas that are just for staff. Rides and attractions are repaired, maintained, and run smoothly. Security cameras are updated and working correctly, arming the company with clear footage that will hold up in court if lawsuits arise. (When I took over as CEO of Boomers, each park was equipped with around a hundred security cameras, but only a few dozen actually worked.) They make sure every member of the team is approaching safety policies to the best of their ability. When a staff member falls short, they address them immediately to provide warnings or additional training so no one gets hurt. No stone goes unturned in the quest for safety compliance.

All of these efforts combine to keep insurance rates low for the business. Claims are few and far between, and the company is able to maintain a solid reputation. Press and reviews about the business are generally positive. When people google the company, they're met with information that inspires trust rather than articles about accidents, injuries, deaths, or complaints. The thought of such issues arising never needs to cross their minds.

What Happens When Safety Is Lacking

Safety problems destroy trust and have the potential to kill a business or brand entirely. Few experiences could be more upsetting to a guest than choosing to come to a place where they or their children could get hurt. This happens more frequently than we think; many companies fall short when it comes to safety and cleanliness.

The biggest issue at companies where safety is lacking is that staff members aren't properly trained to handle emergencies. When an incident happens, they fail to respond appropriately, setting the business up for legal repercussions. The team may also be unaware of how to handle equipment safely, like heavy machinery, drills, knives, or chainsaws. During safety inspections at Boomers, we often found kitchen staff members without cutting gloves, raising the risk of bloody accidents. Tools meant for use by staff may also be left out where children and other guests are walking. The team may not know how to sanitize bathrooms, kitchens, or other areas, resulting in foul smells, mold, or bacterial infections. They may skip precautions that prevent people from getting sick, like emptying full trash cans or washing their hands thoroughly. Injuries and illnesses are likely to occur under such circumstances.

Lax enforcement of safety and cleanliness can also give staff the impression that ongoing maintenance and repair are low-priority tasks. Rides and attractions may break down, get stuck, or malfunction in other ways on a frequent basis. Foliage may grow out of control, setting guests up to trip over roots or get scratched by stray branches. Cracked tiles and uneven concrete may line the floors, causing guests to trip or lose their balance. Paint may be faded, chipped, or lack proper coating. Locks on doors may be broken, creating privacy and security concerns. Fences may be absent, which means guests are allowed into areas they shouldn't be. Issues don't get taken care of until they're already out of hand, leading to complaints. This all creates the impression of a shabby, poorly run business whose owners don't care about guests or their comfort.

Safe businesses monitor guests in all locations and keep them from engaging in dangerous behavior. When this doesn't happen, guests are left to roam free and act in ways that put themselves or others at risk. Children are allowed to climb on furniture or surfaces they shouldn't. Adults who have been served too much alcohol are free to walk around intoxicated. People run or engage in reckless behavior around pools and other areas with water, increasing risk of a drowning incident. Guests fall at attractions like rock-climbing walls or sustain injuries at playgrounds. In other words, the inmates are left in charge of the asylum.

Businesses that slack on safety can also fail to take environmental factors into account. High temperatures heat up metal seats or slides, heightening the risk of burns. Pipes can freeze in cold areas, limiting access to running water. Areas with typhoons, hurricanes, and tornados can be dangerous when furniture is unsecured. These all become hazards unless management comes up with policies and procedures to deal with them.

Security cameras are a key safety investment often overlooked by businesses that want to keep costs low. This is a huge mistake. Any company open to the public will eventually encounter a lawsuit of some kind, and without footage capturing the actions of guests and staff, the court system will have a hard time determining what happened. If you think installing and maintaining security cameras is expensive, just wait until you get sued! Lawsuits are likely to drive up costs in the long run if the company is held liable. Good cameras can prevent this and protect the reputation of the brand.

Implementing Safety as a Core Value

No amount of money should ever stand in the way of safety and cleanliness. It is always worth it, financially speaking, to invest in measures that prevent accidents and injuries. If the seat belts on a ride need replacing, for instance, shut it down until new ones can be installed. Try to anticipate what kind of funding you'll need each quarter and make room in the budget to cover it. Never skimp on these necessary expenses in the name of keeping costs low. Even if a short-term fix is all you can presently afford, go for it. Do what you can.

Be a guest at your business.

Generally speaking, the best way to improve safety and cleanliness at a company is to see the business through the eyes of a guest. Walk around and ask yourself, "What will they see?" Take photos of every issue that needs to be addressed. Are there wooden benches with splinters sticking out? Chipped paint on walls? Overgrown foliage that could scratch or poke someone? Ripped carpets? Broken lights? The first thing I did when I took over Boomers Parks was have insurance brokers walk through each park with me to assess potential safety concerns. Adhering to their advice and requests helped us keep insurance premiums low, which made all the difference.

Focus on your five senses as you experience your business in the way a guest would:

- What do you *see*? Are your attractions displayed clearly, unobstructed by foliage or other objects? Is there signage and clear paths indicating where guests are meant to walk?

- What do you *hear*? Is your music playing at a reasonable volume? Is your sound system up to date and functioning properly? It's difficult for guests and team members to respond to instructions relayed over a loudspeaker if they can't hear them clearly.

- What do you *smell*? Do your bathrooms smell like sewage? They shouldn't. Are the dining areas filled with enticing aromas that encourage guests to stay longer and eat there? Always avoid off-putting smells in favor of appealing ones.

- What do you *taste* when you try the food and drinks sold at your business? Are the alcoholic beverages too strong, too weak, or just right? Are the meals being prepared according to the policies of your restaurants?

- How do things feel when you *touch* them? Are surfaces smooth and safe rather than jagged? Are the temperatures safe for guests or likely to cause burns? Is the ground even and accessible where guests walk?

Managers and team members can stay alert to safety hazards by habitually taking time to experience the business as guests do. Walk around, ride the rides, eat the food, play the games, park in the parking lot, and observe everything around you as you do. There's always something to notice.

Invest in good security cameras.

In our litigious society, you may encounter people who attempt to make false claims against your company. Installing security cameras around each of your locations is an easy way to prove you and your team follow proper safety procedures. Guests are often found liable for incidents due to their own bad behavior. They may hop a fence, end up in an unsafe area, and get hurt. Nine times out of ten, showing proof of recklessness on the part of a guest will get a case dropped. This not only protects the assets of your business but also gives you a chance to review what happened so you can prevent similar events from happening again in the future. "What can we do differently next time?"

During the COVID-19 pandemic, we had to close our parks at Boomers, and unfortunately, people broke in to steal tools and other assets. Luckily, we caught those crimes on tape and were able to review the footage and improve our security systems. Occasionally, employees or even managers are found liable for theft at work. We once caught a group of our guys at Boomers selling go-kart parts out the back door. Imagine our shock to discover this was the cause of our unexplained cost discrepancies in that department! Without cameras, problems like theft often fly under the radar, resulting in higher expenses.

Train employees properly and frequently.

Most safety risks can be avoided if employees are trained well and often. They should have all the knowledge and support they need to respond appropriately to hazardous situations. When best practices are updated, your staff should be too. This should be a regular item on the agenda at daily, weekly, and monthly meetings. Here are some major points to teach while training staff:

- Never over-serve alcohol to guests. If someone is acting intoxicated, it's time to cut them off. Additionally, guests who look young must show proof of legal age to buy alcohol. Watch out for guests who may be high on drugs as well and prevent them from entering areas like pools.

- Utilize proper lifting techniques, wear supportive weight-lifting belts, and use hand carts while lifting heavy objects to avoid back injuries. Learn how to operate machines like forklifts and keep them maintained at all times. If you need help, ask.

- Monitor the behavior of guests on rides, at games, and at attractions like rock-climbing walls where people can get hurt. Keep an eye on them to ensure no one is acting recklessly or putting anyone at risk of injury. Erratic or suspicious behavior should be dealt with head-on. Don't hesitate to call the police if guests break the law or behave aggressively.

- Keep cash drawers minimal and drop extra cash into safes if any are available. Close all stores in pairs when possible and lock all doors promptly, especially after dark.

- Know the exits and evacuation routes and keep them clear at all times. Be familiar with numbers for emergency contacts like police and fire departments, building security, plumbers, and management. Follow established response plans during emergencies.

- Follow recommended procedures during fire drills, active-shooter drills, or incidents that call for CPR. Use role-play during training sessions to make sure everyone has hands-on experience in responding to emergencies. Train them to identify medical conditions like heat exhaustion, heart attacks, or strokes.

- Hire qualified lifeguards and make sure they're set up to see every single person in the pool or surrounding area. They should be able to monitor every guest and keep them safe at all times. When they need a break, have another lifeguard available to take over. Do not allow guests to run in wet areas where they could slip and fall.

If a team member needs to be recertified in a certain skill or isn't performing to company standards, invest in training them further. Most people you hire will be able to meet the mark, but those who can't shouldn't be on staff.

Deal with environmental threats.

If your business is located in an area prone to heavy or extreme weather, create plans to deal with these factors. Prevent guests from touching hot metal that could burn them when the weather is hot. If there's likely to be water or ice on the ground, take measures to keep people from slipping. Secure all furniture, equipment, and infrastructure so nothing ends up blowing away in strong winds. When it's cold, follow procedures that will keep your pipes from freezing or breaking. Have generators available to provide backup electricity in cases of power outages.

Have supplies on hand for emergencies.

When emergencies occur, you'll need a number of essential supplies on hand to address potential problems. Bottled water and nonperishable food should be stored on-site in case of plumbing issues or circumstances where people are prevented from leaving the grounds. Blankets, flashlights, first aid supplies, and battery-powered radios are necessary too. Have everything you need to help guests during times of crisis until emergency responders can get to you.

Ultimately, metrics like insurance claims, reviews, and repeat customers will provide you with a big-picture view of how safe and clean your business is. When you identify areas for improvement, handle them without delay. When it comes to safety, no news is good news. Prevention will save you from thousands of potential headaches and allow your guests to focus on the fun.

The three core values we've discussed so far—**integrity, accountability,** and **safety**—all influence how team members handle our next core value: **service**. The ability to make guests feel at home at your business can set you apart from all your competitors. Next, we'll explore ways to get them raving to friends and family about your company and bring more traffic through your doors.

Key Takeaways

1. **Safety is the foundation of guest trust and business sustainability.**

   - A safe, clean, and comfortable environment is essential for repeat business, positive reviews, and long-term profitability.

   - Safety is about more than regulatory compliance—it's about creating a hazard-free, welcoming atmosphere that guests can relax in and remember positively.

   - Even one preventable incident can damage reputation, increase insurance costs, and erode customer confidence.

2. **Safety requires proactive, ongoing attention.**

   - Train staff regularly, refresh certifications, and role-play emergency scenarios so responses become second nature.

   - Managers must continually inspect, maintain, and repair facilities—addressing hazards before they cause incidents.

   - Safety also includes sanitation, environmental hazard planning, guest behavior monitoring, and investing in tools like quality security cameras.

3. **Prevention is always cheaper and more effective than reaction.**

   - Anticipate risks by experiencing your business as a guest and addressing issues across all senses—sight, sound, smell, taste, and touch.

   - Allocate budget for maintenance, repairs, and safety upgrades before problems escalate.

   - Have emergency supplies, clear procedures, and trained personnel ready so crises are handled quickly, minimizing harm and liability.

Safety Self-Assessment Survey

Rate each question from 1 to 5.

(1 = Not true at all / 5 = Consistently true)

1. Is safety ever sacrificed for speed, convenience, or revenue?

   Rating: _______

2. Are safety procedures followed consistently during peak pressure and high volume?

   Rating: _______

3. Is safety training ongoing, documented, and reinforced—not just completed once?

   Rating: _______

4. Do team members know emergency procedures, exits, and escalation protocols?

   Rating: _______

5. Are hazards and near misses reported immediately rather than ignored or hidden?

   Rating: _______

6. Are cleanliness and maintenance treated as safety issues, not as cosmetic issues?

   Rating: _______

7. Do leaders regularly inspect safety-critical areas rather than assuming compliance?

   Rating: _______

8. Is unsafe guest behavior addressed promptly and consistently?

   Rating: _______

9. Is equipment removed from service immediately when it fails safety standards?

   Rating: _______

10. Would safety practices withstand regulatory, legal, or public scrutiny if reviewed today?

    Rating: _______

Scoring & Interpretation

- **40–50 (Strong):** Safety is embedded, practiced, and defended under pressure.

- **25–39 (Mixed):** Safety is present but conditional; risk increases during busy periods.

- **10–24 (At Risk):** A serious incident is likely. Leadership must intervene immediately.

Leader Reflection (Answer honestly!)

1. Where have we normalized minor safety shortcuts because "nothing happened"?

2. Would I feel comfortable putting my family in this environment today?

3. Are leaders modeling safety behaviors or just enforcing them when convenient?

4. Do people speak up about hazards, or do they avoid being "the problem"?

5. What is one safety issue we keep postponing that could become catastrophic?

How to Use This Survey

- **Run quarterly and before peak seasons.** Stress reveals weaknesses; prepare ahead of pressure.

- **Use immediately after incidents.** Treat any event as a system signal, not as a one-off mistake.

- **Pair scores with inspections.** Validate perceptions with actual walk-throughs and documentation checks.

- **Close the loop.** Translate low scores into specific corrective actions: training refreshers, audits, equipment repairs, staffing changes.

- **Make safety visible.** Create routines (pre-shift checks, incident reviews, hazard reporting expectations) that reinforce safety daily.

4. Service
Making People Feel Seen

Whatever you do, do it well. Do it so well that when people see you do it,
they will want to come back and see you do it again, and
they will want to bring others and show them how well you do what you do.

—Walt Disney

When I worked at Walt Disney World in Orlando, I learned what top-notch service looked like. Disney staff members refer to customers as "guests," just like any friend you would invite into your home. The parks run like an improvised play starring both the actors (the staff) and the audience (the guests). You won't see members of the team scrolling on their phones or napping during shifts. They're "on" from the moment they appear in front of guests, and they stay in character until they're offstage. This provides guests with a fully immersive experience. They're transported to a magical, inspiring land where impossible dreams come true. Every member of the Disney team works to sustain that suspension of belief during their interactions with guests, creating an experience that can't be found anywhere else. Disney stands out as a world-class company because its team is trained to go above and beyond to maintain brand standards in front of guests.

Great customer service is about crafting a fun, memorable, welcoming experience for every guest who walks through your door. At a minimum, they should be able to feel comfortable and leave their worries behind while they're at your business. If you can provide a joyful, awe-inspiring, truly unique experience that will have them raving about your company for days, that's ideal. The key difference between a good customer experience and a great one is a service-focused team trained to prioritize the comfort and feelings of guests. Implementing service as a core value at your business can help your team focus on working together to provide the memorable experience your brand aims to create.

What Service Looks Like in Business

At Dad's business, the Spirit of '76, service meant remembering a regular's order or slipping an extra cherry on a sundae for a kid who lost at mini golf. At EPCOT, service meant speed, warmth, and consistency, even when the line stretched to tomorrow. You learned the rhythm: two trays, three greetings, a check on the family with a stroller. Guests might forget what you said, but they never forget how you made them feel.

When a business is failing, service is often the first casualty. When I first took over at Boomers, I walked into locations where no one smiled, tables sat sticky, and the only words you heard were "we're short-staffed." So, I grabbed a rag and a bin. I bussed, wiped, delivered food, and thanked people by name. Managers followed. The change wasn't in a memo—it was in modeling. When leaders serve, teams serve. When teams serve, guests return. And revenue follows.

Businesses with great service know how to make their customers feel welcome. Their teams act as if they're happy to see each customer and help them get what they came for quickly and efficiently. Employees must be able to put aside their own feelings and focus on the needs of the guests, anticipating those needs when possible. They may not feel enthusiastic about work every day, but they can at least say, "Hey, I'm breathing, and I'm getting paid. It could be worse." We all have to set our feelings aside to build success in our careers by focusing on the collective mission of the company.

Team members who embrace service as a core value are habitually present and engaged with what's happening around them. When they see guests, they smile and say hello. They ask what people need and communicate effectively. When they see a task that needs to be taken care of, they take the initiative and get it done without waiting to be asked. Helping others brings them satisfaction.

Employees who provide great service are cognizant of the fact that every guest has problems to deal with in their life. They've got worries, obligations, stressors, and personal baggage. These guests come to businesses to forget about those worries and have someone else make life easier for them for a while. They may have just worked a sixty-hour week and only have one night—the night they come to your business— to spend with their family. They may have recently experienced a death in the family or been the victim of a serious crime. Service-minded employees understand that everyone desires respect and kindness. The best thing they can do is keep everyone feeling positive and welcome.

Fast-food chain Chick-fil-A is an example of a successful business that embraces service as a core value. They have a tradition where team members answer, "My pleasure," whenever a customer thanks them. They want to give the impression that every employee is happy to be there helping others feel good. The company's founder, Samuel Truett Cathy, started the business envisioning a restaurant where customers could come for a chicken sandwich and receive premium service. He would walk around tables talking to guests and getting to know them. These personal interactions made his place memorable, proving that even a cheap meal can be sold as a premium experience when team members embody top-notch service.

Service-minded employees also explain to guests what they need to know in order to have the best experience possible. Servers at restaurants talk about the specials and tip guests off to the most popular dishes on the menu. At theme parks, team members help guests who look lost find their way and give advice on how to avoid long wait times. At video game stores, team members can allow customers free trials to see if they like certain games enough to purchase them. If they see a guest is upset, they ask whether there's anything they can do to help. And if the company has changed a policy or is implementing a new campaign, they spread the word to ensure guests know what's up. Clarity is kindness.

Guests should never be left confused or frustrated about policies team members can easily explain.

Repeat guests are the goal. The more a business can do to create an exceptional experience, the less time and effort they have to spend hunting for new guests. Brands with great service become a household name by generating loyalty among their customer base—especially locals. If you can become their go-to destination for leisure, you'll be able to keep sales up, even during hard times.

A business absolutely devoted to service will have only one worry about profits. They will be embarrassingly large.

—Henry Ford

What Happens When Service Is Lacking

A lack of great service at a business leaves a horrible impression and makes guests less likely to return in the future. Why choose a place with rude, disinterested staff when they could go somewhere else for a better experience? You want them to choose *you* above anyone else in the community, and they'll be unlikely to do so if they've had a bad time or heard other people complaining about service at your company.

Employees who aren't trained in customer service tend to be too focused on themselves and their own feelings to properly focus on guests. Guests may be left waiting for service for several minutes, wondering when someone will finally come and assist them. Poorly trained employees may also act timidly, failing to greet guests or to check in with them about their needs. They don't see things from a guest's point of view or care enough to take the initiative to jump in and solve problems. Occasionally, you may even get employees with serious attitude problems who offend guests or act like being at work is an inconvenience. Everyone has bad days, but when this is impacting a guest's experience, it reflects poorly on the company.

Thanks to the influence of social media and internet addiction, it's common these days for people to dissociate from what's in front of them. When employees aren't used to connecting with strangers, they may not understand how important it is to create positive emotions between themselves and guests. If members of your team don't greet guests with a smile and acknowledge their humanity, your brand will feel cold and lifeless. It's alienating to walk into a business and be met with blank stares.

Businesses with bad customer service also tend to do a poor job of communicating with guests. They don't put up signage when necessary or update their website about policy changes or offerings. They may close a location without updating their business settings on Google. Customers may drive from long distances, thinking the place will be open, only to arrive and discover they've wasted their time. Guests will be in the dark about special events, celebrations, or membership plans. This lack of communication results in confusion, frustration, and missed opportunities.

When a company is characterized by bad service, guests start to complain and leave bad reviews. This can tank the reputation of the business online. People who google it will be met with terrible stories and warnings by others to stay away. Word gets around when people leave a business with a bad taste in their mouths. They want to give others a heads-up so people can avoid supporting companies that fail to prioritize the people who generate their profits, and rightfully so.

Implementing Service as a Core Value

Great service is the result of thorough onboarding and training programs. Warmth and attentiveness don't always come naturally to employees, especially those working their first or second job. They need leaders to explain and demonstrate how to create a seamless and comfortable experience for guests. Once they understand what's expected of them, they can start working to align their service skills with company standards. As a manager, supervisor, or representative from the corporate office, there are a number of things you can do to help employees create the best experience possible for guests.

Train employees to facilitate escapism.

Guests want to escape their problems and worries when they're out at a business. They don't want to experience bad feelings or encounter any difficulties that will make their life less pleasant. With great customer service training, your team can help them in their quest for escapism. What will it take to get the minds of guests off the ills of the world?

For many people, everyday life tends to be challenging, abrasive, and a bit boring. To create positive memories, the ambience at your business should exceed this standard. Have your employees ask themselves these questions:

- **How can I make things easy for guests while they're here?** They shouldn't have to think too much or ask questions to figure out what to do next. Do they look confused? Do they know where they're going? Is it their first time? Do they need help getting oriented?

- **How can I make guests feel comfortable?** Focus on their five senses. Is the temperature in the room hot, cold, or just right? Is it too noisy or loud? Is there adequate seating for everyone? Does the food taste good?

- **How can I elevate the mood?** Happiness is infectious. Are the employees smiling and contributing to a light atmosphere? Can they make guests laugh? Are there games for kids to play?

Anticipate the needs of guests.

Attentive employees keep their eyes on guests so they can jump in right when they're needed and make the experience better. They observe the guest's mood, who they're with, and what they might want. A parent visiting the business with their child, for instance, will be highly invested in keeping their kid happy and tantrum free. Employees can assist in entertaining the child by offering crayons and paper or toys for them to play with. A guest who has just been exercising or out in the sun will need water. Guests who have just been swimming will need access to clean towels. Elderly guests may need help opening doors or moving chairs. It's your team's job to notice and help with all these issues as they arise.

To provide truly world-class service that goes above and beyond expectations, train your employees to be on the lookout for opportunities to delight your guests with thoughtful surprises. A married couple visiting the business on their anniversary could be offered a complimentary bottle of champagne, for example. A guest who's in a bad mood after a losing streak at your arcade could be given extra tokens to play with. If a guest is having a birthday, your team could offer a free dessert. If a guest is visiting from overseas, you might recommend a local specialty they won't be able to try anywhere else. These personal touches make guests feel seen and valued, which, in turn, makes them more likely to remember you.

Explain things clearly to employees so they can explain them to guests.

If your team is confused or unclear about what's happening at your business, they'll have a hard time explaining your policies to guests. This can cause issues that lead to complaints, so it's important to keep your employees informed and aware. If you do retail, for instance, educate all employees on your return policy. Get them all up to speed on the rules you ask guests to follow and the reasoning behind each of them, if necessary. Train them on how to instruct and guide guests in case of an emergency. Use role-play to help them practice articulating what they need to say. This will make it easier for them to handle situations well in the heat of the moment.

It can take our minds time and repetition to absorb new information. It's not enough to explain something once and expect your team to remember and master it. You must explain things over and over, using different words, examples, and tools. You can use quotes, role-play activities, written guides, infographics, pictures, Q&A sessions, and many other techniques to teach employees how to provide exceptional service. Continually make your standards known and give staff ideas for ways to meet those expectations. The more engaged you are with them, the more engaged they will be with guests. Clear explanation and open communication should be everyday aspects of your company culture.

Respond to feedback and reviews.

When you receive a one- or two-star review on Google, it's important to follow up not only with the guest who complained but with staff as well. The public will let you know about whatever problems your business has with service, often in detail. Taking their complaints up with the team will help you collectively refine your approach. Perhaps they were frustrated by what they interpreted as rude or dismissive behavior. Does a particular employee need to be retrained, or is it an issue with the whole team? Are your employees making eye contact, smiling, and listening attentively to guests? Do they follow through on helping the guests who approach them for assistance? Do they take guests and their concerns seriously in a way that's visible? Is there empathy? Most negative reviews are blown out of proportion by angry guests, but some represent a legitimate opportunity for improvement. If you see a pattern—for example, similar complaints following events like birthday parties—there's definitely an issue that needs to be addressed. Put that feedback to use rather than shrugging it off.

If you work at the corporate office, go visit different locations.

I've known many C-suite executives who never left the corporate office to check out what was happening at the company's branch locations. Consequently, they had no idea what kinds of experiences customers and employees were having. When I took over as CEO at Boomers Parks, I would randomly show up unannounced at each location to assess how things were going on the ground. I didn't do this to look for problems or breathe down anyone's neck. I simply wanted to get a pulse on what was actually taking place at the business. How busy were the parks on weekdays versus weekends? How were team members behaving when the parks were crowded versus when they were slow? Were they paying attention to guests? Did the place look clean? Were they following protocol? Getting out of the office so you can see what's happening is the best way to be a guest and see what they see.

Hold service-focused meetings before shifts.

It never hurts to meet with your team before their shift to highlight what you're looking to achieve with guests. Even if they've mastered the basics, things are constantly changing, and they'll need updates. Are you expecting the day to be busy? Have there been any incidents lately? Do you have any relevant anecdotes to share with them? Are there any new products on offer? How are sales this week? What's happening in other departments? Are any of your rides or attractions out of order? What are the specials at the restaurant? What's the weather forecast predicting, and how might that impact everyone's day? Putting aside a few minutes before employees start their shifts gives you and your managers a window to check in about little points like this. You can also use this time to prime them for good conversations with guests. Do you have any special offers on that particular day, like games at half price? Those are great topics to bring up with guests.

Encourage your team to "be the guest."

In the last chapter, I mentioned the importance of seeing your business through the eyes of a guest. Your employees should all be thinking this way too so they can understand how to serve guests better. Have them try your products and services for themselves. Ask them to eat the food, use the guest bathrooms, stand in the lines, play the games, walk around the premises, and then report what they notice. Are there any improvements that could be made? Is maintenance necessary? Are there places where things could be explained better? Opening the door to this kind of feedback from your team will empower you to solve little problems early and often, resulting in a smoother guest experience.

The more your team thinks like a guest, the more in tune they'll be with your customer base. This attunement is the basis of a strong brand presence in your community. With great service, your business will become a local staple that guests love to support because they feel welcome. People want to be a part of something positive and spend time around others in good spirits. You and your team can create that space for them. Be the timeless getaway your community needs.

By now, you may have noticed open communication as a recurring theme. This is, in fact, a core value on its own; no business can run smoothly unless everyone gets on the same page by communicating clearly. We'll talk next about opening up lines of communication between all the nodes of your business.

Key Takeaways

1. **Service creates emotional connections that drive loyalty.**

   - Guests remember how you made them feel more than what you sold them, so service must focus on warmth, attentiveness, and making guests feel valued.

   - A service-driven team anticipates needs, provides thoughtful touches, and helps guests escape from daily stresses, creating memorable experiences that encourage repeat visits.

   - Brands that consistently deliver exceptional service become go-to destinations in their communities, reducing reliance on constant new customer acquisition.

2. **Poor service damages reputation and repels guests.**

   - Rude, disengaged, or inattentive staff leave a lasting negative impression, which can quickly spread through online reviews and word of mouth.

   - Poor communication with guests—including unclear policies, outdated information, and lack of signage—leads to confusion, frustration, and lost business.

   - In today's connected world, negative service experiences are amplified publicly, making service failures more costly than ever.

3. **Service excellence requires training, communication, and immersion.**

   - Train employees to "be the guest" and experience the business from the customer's perspective so they can spot and fix issues before they impact visitors.

   - Hold pre-shift service meetings, keep employees informed, role-play scenarios, and continually reinforce service standards.

   - Use guest feedback and on-site visits by leadership to refine service, ensuring every interaction aligns with brand values and guest expectations.

Service Self-Assessment Survey

Rate each question from 1 to 5.

(1 = Not true at all / 5 = Consistently true)

1. Are guests acknowledged promptly and warmly, with eye contact and a genuine tone?

   Rating: _______

2. Do team members remain present and attentive rather than distracted or disengaged?

   Rating: _______

3. Are guest needs anticipated rather than handled only after frustration builds?

   Rating: _______

4. Are instructions, directions, and explanations delivered clearly to reduce confusion?

   Rating: _______

5. Are guest issues owned through resolution rather than passed along or deferred?

   Rating: _______

6. Is a positive, composed demeanor maintained even under stress or high volume?

   Rating: _______

7. Are personal touches (small gestures that make guests feel seen) encouraged?

   Rating: _______

8. Does cleanliness consistently support guest comfort and confidence?

   Rating: _______

9. Is guest feedback actively used to improve behaviors, not just collected?

   Rating: _______

10. Do leaders model service on the floor by stepping in, helping, and coaching?

   Rating: _______

Scoring & Interpretation

- **40–50 (Strong):** Service is consistent and emotionally resonant; guests feel valued.

- **25–39 (Mixed):** Service varies by person or shift; inconsistency weakens loyalty.

- **10–24 (At Risk):** Service is breaking down; reputation and repeat visits are at risk.

Leader Reflection (Answer honestly!)

1. Do guests feel like the purpose of our work—or an interruption to it?

2. Are we coaching presence and empathy—or only task execution?

3. Where do we allow distractions to sabotage the guest experience?

4. When was the last time I personally served a guest and observed our standards firsthand?

5. What service behavior is tolerated today that will become normal tomorrow?

How to Use This Survey

- **Use before peak periods.** Service cracks appear fastest during periods of high volume, stress, and staffing shortages.

- **Pair with observation.** Validate scores through on-floor walks and guest journey reviews.

- **Coach in the moment.** Service improves fastest with real-time correction and reinforcement.

- **Use feedback strategically.** Link low-scoring questions to guest complaints, reviews, and return rates.

- **Model from leadership.** Leaders must be present and visible; service culture follows leadership behavior.

5. Communication
Clarity Builds Trust

The single biggest problem in communication is the illusion that it has taken place.

—George Bernard Shaw

One of the greatest challenges of turning around a failing business is implementing big changes with existing staff. As the new CEO at Boomers, I did this by communicating with team members at all our locations during daily, weekly, and monthly meetings. I showed them the big picture of how the business was operating and taught them how their role affected our overall success as a company. I translated information about things like private equity investments, which most of them weren't aware of. I discussed what was working, what wasn't, and how we were going to change things in a vernacular they could understand and relay to our guests. Each message I put out to the team was consistent; every employee got the same information. Through open communication, I was able to get their buy-in and see results from the changes we were making within a few weeks.

Businesses function best when all members of the organization share one clear, collective vision. To get everyone on the same page, transparent, open communication must become a core value. Company leaders must be constantly talking about the vision they're aiming for and how everyone can work together to get there. It's not enough to say something once and expect everyone to get it. Policies, updates, and the overall direction of the company must be explained again and again in a variety of ways. Once everyone is operating in sync, that's when the magic starts happening.

What Communication Looks Like in Business

My father never sugarcoated things. If a fence was crooked, he said it. If I cut corners on a job, he pointed it out in front of everyone. That stung, but it taught me the power of direct, clear words. At EPCOT, I saw the same in a different form: morning huddles before opening. Leaders laid out the flow—who worked registers, who handled trays, who rotated breaks. Ten minutes of clarity saved ten hours of chaos. I also learned the cost of poor communication. One night in Cash Control, a deposit bag went "missing." Panic spread until someone admitted they had moved it without telling anyone. A two-minute heads-up would have saved two hours of fear.

When I first arrived at Boomers years later as the company's new CEO, leaders communicated through rumors. Operators found out about changes from the grapevine, not from the top. I ended that fast. Every week, I sent a Monday update: numbers, wins, losses, next week's focus. No spin. Just clarity. We also trained managers to hold daily stand-ups and weekly check-ins. Did it fix everything overnight? No. But it rewired the culture. Rumor gave way to rhythm. People stopped asking, "What's happening?" and started saying, "Here's what's next." That shift fueled momentum.

Open communication is the status quo at companies that manage to get everyone collaborating to create the same vision. Employees and managers speak about company expectations and goals continuously rather than occasionally. Managers talk with the corporate office about what's happening on the ground at their locations. Everyone is taught to see how their specific role fits into the big picture and what they can do to keep the business profitable. They own their part and willingly take part in transparent conversations about what needs to be done, especially while changes are being enacted. Change is the only constant in life, and ideally, employees can anticipate this and pivot together by discussing their common goals.

When managers and other company leaders embrace communication as a core value, they learn to explain *why* a change is happening in detail. They articulate the reason behind every big decision and how it relates to each employee. They work to earn the buy-in of their team so each member can start taking ownership for the role they play. When company leaders see the needle isn't moving and hit a wall, they keep engaging the team to create change because they know the survival of the business depends on it. Giving up is not an option.

Constructive feedback is an integral aspect of communication as a core value. Decisions are made from the top down, but feedback is elicited as the team works through challenges and changes together. When problems arise, people feel empowered to speak up about them, taking accountability for their part in the issue when necessary. Everyone is kept informed about challenges the company is facing in relation to guest incidents, profits and losses, compliance with local laws, and other big-picture concerns.

When communication is commonplace, problems are individually analyzed and addressed so their sources can be identified. Lazy blanket changes aren't enforced across the board unless patterns are observed consistently. Financial discrepancies, for instance, may be the result of one employee's mistake rather than a systemic issue. When an employee isn't performing well, they're warned, retrained, and given opportunities to improve when appropriate. When someone must be fired, the reason is clear. No one is blindsided by a disciplinary action. Staff members are made aware and routinely reminded of the brand standards they're expected to meet.

The core value of communication applies to customers as well. Customers should never be in the dark about things they need to know at a business. They're informed of programs, policies, and offerings. They're told where they have to go and what they have to do in order to make the most of their experience. When they have questions or concerns, team members are able to answer, explain, and articulate in detail. They feel seen, heard, and valued by everyone they encounter from the business.

What Happens When Communication Is Lacking

Like a human being, a company has to have an internal communication mechanism, a "nervous system," to coordinate its actions.

—Bill Gates

A business without open communication and transparency is bound to crash and burn. The shared vision intended for the team is likely unclear, if one has been defined by its owners in the first place. There's no collective focus on what needs to be done, and the goals of the team are hazy. Company leaders are worried about taking risks and don't want employees knowing the big picture of how the business works, so employees are clueless about how their role fits into and impacts the organization. Important information about the company isn't shared or explained to them, leading to confusion and frustration during conversations with guests.

It's incredibly difficult to make company-wide changes without clear, thorough, routine communication at all levels. Managers and other employees are resistant to changing how things are done when they're unaware of the reason for it. They're unlikely to buy into the process if it all feels arbitrary. Leaders at a company may explain the changes they want to see once or twice and then hit a wall when progress isn't made. They can't identify the source of the problem because employees don't feel they can speak up about problems when open, two-way communication isn't happening.

Communication also needs to happen if employees are to improve when they're not meeting company standards. Without clear, constructive feedback, people can't make the specific changes their superiors want to see. They may feel surprised by a bad performance review if they haven't received enough guidance about how to do better before that point. In extreme cases, this can lead to allegations of wrongful termination. Managers with poor communication skills may struggle to keep employees aware of their status at the company.

When communication and transparency aren't up to par at a business, guests tend to be the most confused of all. There may not be signage to point them in the right direction. They may be confused on where to go or what to do. *"Should I seat myself or wait for someone to seat me? Sure feels awkward standing here…"* Employees don't help them out or inform them of current offerings, deals, or memberships. Opportunities for connection and upselling are missed.

Implementing Communication as a Core Value

Open communication is all about meeting and talking with colleagues and customers without the need for secrecy or anxiety. Transparency creates clarity for everyone, cuts down on confusion, and creates trust. Here are some tips for implementing this core value:

Describe the vision in detail on a regular basis.

One of the most powerful ways to implement communication as a core value is to consistently articulate where the company is going and what it stands for. That means describing the vision not just once but regularly, in vivid and memorable ways. During onboarding, training sessions, team meetings, and even casual check-ins, take time to paint a clear picture of what success looks like. Don't assume people just "get it" after hearing it once. Instead, repeat the vision often, using different formats to make it stick: Share a relevant anecdote, highlight a quote that captures your values, show a photo or video that illustrates a key goal, or role-play a scenario that brings the vision to life.

The more often people hear and see the vision, the more likely they are to internalize it and act accordingly. And this isn't just the job of the founder or top executive. Every manager should be expected to carry the vision forward by regularly checking in with their teams. Daily huddles, weekly updates, and monthly deep dives all help keep the message fresh and aligned across levels. When everyone is speaking the same language and aiming for the same target, communication becomes a tool for unity and momentum.

Always explain the "why."

One of the most important habits you and your managers can develop is explaining why decisions are being made. It's not enough to tell people what to do. They need to understand the reasoning behind it. Why are prices going up? Why are short pre-shift meetings being added? Why is there a new policy around uniforms or scheduling? Each of these changes may seem small, but without context, they can easily feel arbitrary. When people don't understand the purpose behind a decision, they're less likely to support it.

Explaining the "why" helps people shift their mindset. It builds trust, clarifies priorities, and makes change feel purposeful rather than imposed. When employees understand what a change is meant to accomplish, they're far more likely to get on board. Even better, invite your team to articulate the reasoning in their own words. When people can explain a policy change themselves, it shows they've truly internalized it. That's when communication turns into culture.

Ask for feedback from the team.

Communication works best when it's not just top-down but truly two-way. One of the most effective ways to embed communication as a core value is to actively seek feedback from your team, especially when introducing new policies or navigating change. Invite people to share their thoughts, concerns, and ideas. This isn't about avoiding resistance; it's about understanding it. When team members push back, it's often because they don't fully understand the rationale. Instead of dismissing that resistance, treat it as valuable input. Ask clarifying questions. Listen without defensiveness. Modify how you explain your decisions based on what people need to hear, not just on what you want to say.

Whenever possible, anticipate common concerns and come prepared with thoughtful responses. Better yet, engage your team early by prompting them to think about solutions themselves. Try asking, "What could you do differently at your location to address this issue?" When people are part of the problem-solving process, they feel a sense of ownership, which leads to stronger buy-in and better results.

Don't give up when you hit a wall.

Even when communication is clear, consistent, and thoughtful, change doesn't happen overnight. People need time to absorb new policies, shift their habits, and understand the "why" behind what's being asked of them. When your message doesn't seem to be landing or progress feels slower than expected, it's easy to get discouraged. Implementing communication as a core value means committing to it, even when you feel like you're repeating yourself or hitting a wall. Don't pull back. Lean in. Keep engaging with your team, asking questions, listening to their concerns, and creating space for real dialogue. Sometimes, people aren't resisting the message—they're just trying to make sense of it, or they need more context, support, or time. Meet your team where they are. Reinforce the goals, clarify expectations, and invite input on what's working and what's not. When people feel heard and included in the process, they're far more likely to take ownership and help move the needle.

Keep everyone in the know.

Transparency is a key ingredient in building a culture of strong communication. While it's important to respect personal privacy and sensitive information, leaders should default to openness whenever possible, especially when decisions or events affect the broader team. For example, imagine there's a theft incident involving a customer, and new procedures are implemented as a result. While it might seem natural to share the update only with the loss prevention or security staff, keeping the entire team informed reinforces a sense of shared responsibility. It allows everyone to understand the "why" behind the policy shift and encourages vigilance and cohesion across departments.

When employees are consistently kept in the loop, they're more likely to feel valued, trusted, and empowered to act in alignment with the company's goals. Communication isn't just about sending messages. It's about building context and clarity so people can make better decisions together.

Give specific feedback so people can perform better.

Communication as a core value doesn't just mean keeping people informed. It also means helping them grow. One of the most powerful ways to do that is by giving specific, constructive feedback that supports better performance. Employees, especially those who are new to the workforce, may not always recognize what's holding them back from meeting expectations. Vague critiques like "do better" or "this isn't working" can leave people feeling frustrated or confused. Instead, offer clear, actionable observations: Describe what you're seeing, explain why it matters, and suggest how to improve, such as "I noticed you've been late to your shift a few times this week. Being on time is important because it helps the whole team stay on track. Let's talk about what's getting in the way and how we can fix it."

If you're still not seeing improvement, don't let silence fill the gap. Document concerns through written warnings and invite the employee to cocreate a plan for getting back on track. Communication should always be a two-way street rooted in clarity, respect, and a shared commitment to growth.

Open lines of communication with guests.

There are many ways to communicate with customers to improve their experience at your business. Where they need to go and what they need to do should always be clear. For instance, in order to manage your crowds, you'll want a controlled entry and exit plan that ensures all guests come in through one entrance and leave through another. You can achieve this with signage on the ground and throughout your location. Install directories, like the ones placed throughout malls, to help them find their way around. Encourage guests to leave feedback online or via email, especially if they've had a good experience. People feel more valued when you speak directly to them and ask for their opinion.

There are countless ways to facilitate communication at a business. Getting creative will enable you to get your employees, guests, managers, and everyone at the corporate office in alignment about company goals.

Clear, open communication sets the foundation for trust, but it's commitment that builds on that foundation and turns words into action. Once expectations have been expressed, it's the follow-through that defines a company's integrity. In the next chapter, we'll explore how commitment deepens alignment, drives accountability, and transforms communication into lasting impact.

Key Takeaways

1. **Clear, consistent, and transparent communication aligns the entire organization.**

   - Businesses run best when everyone understands the vision and goals and their role in achieving them.

   - Leaders must repeat key messages often, explain the "why" behind decisions, and ensure every level of the company—from corporate to frontline—shares the same understanding.

   - Two-way communication builds trust and buy-in, especially during times of change.

2. **Poor communication breeds confusion, resistance, and missed opportunities.**

   - Without clear explanations, employees may resist changes, feel disconnected from the company's goals, or fail to meet standards.

   - Guests suffer when information is incomplete—causing frustration, negative reviews, and lost sales.

   - Leaders who fail to provide timely feedback or transparency risk lowering performance and morale.

3. **Communication must be active, ongoing, and inclusive.**

   - Solicit feedback, listen without defensiveness, and adjust your message based on what people need to hear.

   - Keep employees and guests informed with clear instructions, visible signage, updated policies, and proactive outreach.

   - Use specific, constructive feedback to guide performance improvements and ensure both internal teams and customers feel heard and valued.

Communication Self-Assessment Survey

Rate each question from 1 to 5.

(1 = Not true at all / 5 = Consistently true)

1. Are vision and priorities communicated consistently—not just occasionally?

   Rating: ______

2. Are key decisions explained with context, including the "why" behind them?

   Rating: ______

3. Does information flow clearly from leadership to managers and managers to frontline teams?

   Rating: ______

4. Do managers hold regular alignment meetings or huddles to reinforce expectations?

   Rating: ______

5. Do employees feel safe asking questions and seeking clarity without being judged?

   Rating: ______

6. Is feedback specific, timely, and actionable rather than vague or delayed?

   Rating: ______

7. Are rumors addressed directly with facts rather than allowed to spread?

   Rating: ______

8. Do employees understand how their role impacts the bigger mission and results?

   Rating: ______

9. Do guests receive clear, consistent information that reduces confusion and frustration?

   Rating: _______

10. Do leaders confirm understanding by asking people to repeat back priorities and expectations?

    Rating: _______

Scoring & Interpretation

- **40–50 (Strong):** The organization is aligned; execution is faster, and friction is lower.

- **25–39 (Mixed):** Messages exist, but understanding varies; misalignment creates drag.

- **10–24 (At Risk):** Communication is breaking down; confusion and rumor are undermining execution.

Leader Reflection (Answer honestly!)

1. Where have I assumed understanding rather than confirming it?
2. Are my messages repeated enough to become cultural memory—or just delivered once?
3. Do people hear consistent priorities, or do priorities shift based on the week?
4. Do employees trust leadership communication, or do they rely on rumor?
5. Do I listen as intentionally as I speak?

How to Use This Survey

- **Use after change.** Apply after reorganizations, launches, new strategies, or policy shifts.

- **Compare levels.** Run it across leadership, managers, and frontline teams to reveal gaps in understanding.

- **Improve cadence.** Translate low scores into structured communication routines (daily huddles, weekly updates, monthly reviews).

- **Confirm understanding.** Build "repeat back" into meetings to validate clarity.

- **Simplify priorities.** If scores are low, reduce competing messages and emphasize two or three priorities repeatedly.

6. Commitment
Staying the Course When It Gets Hard

There's a difference between interest and commitment. When you're interested in doing something, you do it only when it's convenient. When you're committed to something, you accept no excuses—only results.

—Ken Blanchard

As a turnaround specialist, I have to go all-in on a failing business to make it profitable. When I take on a new project, whether it's a theme park or a family entertainment center, I live and breathe it from day one. I'll often find myself up late, energized by ideas to fix the company's biggest issues. It's incredibly motivating to improve a workplace for a team that wants to succeed, but turnarounds are never easy. When COVID-19 hit the United States, the company I was working with had to close all its locations and lost every dollar of revenue. Reopening brought a whole new wave of challenges. Guests were hesitant to return, employees were unsure if it was safe, and every step forward seemed to come with a step back. We were in uncharted territory, making decisions as we learned more about the virus in real time. In moments like that, success hinges on one thing: commitment. Without the unwavering dedication of the team—and my own—the business wouldn't have made it.

Commitment, in addition to integrity, is a core value that fuels all the others in this book. It's the passion and persistence to stand by the company's mission through both calm and crisis. It's the promise not to walk away when things get hard but to stay engaged, adapt, and push forward. Without commitment, even the clearest strategy can't take root. Great leaders know how to inspire that same dedication in others, rallying teams and sustaining momentum through the toughest times. Without commitment—especially from leadership—everything else rests on shaky ground.

What Commitment Looks Like in Business

When I worked at EPCOT as a teenager, and the park emptied at the end of the night, we still had hours of cleaning, stocking, and counting ahead. Many employees bolted at the first chance. I stayed. Commitment wasn't glamorous—it was sweeping and mopping floors at 1 or 2 a.m. or coming back the next day sore but ready. It meant sticking with a job even when the fun part was long over.

My manager at Disney was named Frank, and he was one of the most disciplined, precise leaders I've ever worked with. He never raised his voice or micromanaged, but you always knew the standard. If financial statements were due at 8 a.m., he expected them done at that time and no later. If a variance was off by even a small fraction, he expected us to understand why, not guess. One morning, after a chaotic week, I turned in a report with a glaring mistake. Frank called me into his office. He didn't scold me. He simply slid the report across the desk and asked, "Tim, is this your best work?"

I swallowed hard, seeing what I'd done wrong. "No, it's not."

He nodded. "Then let's not make it a habit."

That moment stuck with me. Not because of the mistake, but because of his quiet, unwavering commitment to excellence. He didn't shame me. He lifted the standard and expected me to rise with it. I corrected the report immediately and never made that same mistake again. Frank taught me something foundational while I worked for him: Commitment is not about intensity but consistency. It didn't require loud, dramatic heroics or last-minute sprints. Instead, it required me to show up every day with discipline, accuracy, and pride in my work, even when I didn't feel like it.

Years later at Boomers, when I inherited a company losing ten million dollars a year, my commitment was tested more deeply. There were nights I lay awake wondering if turning the company around was even possible and days spent fighting declining morale and disastrous financials. It would've been easier to quit, cut my losses, and walk away. But commitment means showing up again tomorrow, even when the spreadsheet screams failure. We built trust one week at a time. We celebrated small wins—costs down 1 percent, birthday parties booked ahead of pace, a safety audit cleared. String enough of those together, and suddenly you're climbing again rather than falling. That climb required stubborn, gritty commitment.

When a team is truly committed, there's no hesitation about whether the job will get done. It's simply a matter of *how*. Committed employees approach their work with focus, resilience, and a can-do attitude. They don't back down when a task is difficult or unfamiliar. Instead, they push forward, ask for help when needed, and collaborate to find solutions. Giving up isn't on the table. These employees are genuinely invested in the company's purpose, values, and goals. They're not just clocking in and out. They want to be part of something meaningful. You can see it in their energy: They greet guests with a smile, support their teammates, and stay positive even when the day gets tough. Their satisfaction comes from making things better—improving processes, solving problems, and creating memorable experiences. That sense of purpose fuels their performance.

When commitment is deeply rooted as a core value, it's reflected at every level of the organization. Managers and leaders model that same dedication, upholding company policies and embodying the values they expect from their teams. They also hire with intention, seeking out people who bring the right mindset and work ethic to the table. Because they know that even one person who lacks commitment can undermine morale and momentum. A single disengaged employee can quickly become a drag on an otherwise high-performing team.

Committed leaders go beyond enforcing rules. They work to empower their teams to take ownership. They foster an environment where employees feel trusted, supported, and equipped to make decisions, even when leadership isn't around. That kind of empowerment builds resilience and ensures the business keeps moving forward, no matter what challenges arise.

Commit to your business. Believe in it more than anybody else.

—Sam Walton

What Happens When Commitment Is Lacking

When commitment is missing in an organization, it shows. Team members who lack commitment are there for a paycheck, not a purpose, and they have no attachment to the job. They haven't bought into the company's values and couldn't care less about its success. Instead of taking ownership, they do the bare minimum or less. Tasks get skipped, corners are cut, and the attitude they bring to work reflects it. They may show up late, act disengaged, and seem visibly unhappy to be there.

Uncommitted team members also tend to focus on problems rather than solutions. Instead of asking, "How can we fix this?" they default to saying, "This won't work," or "That's not my job." They complain frequently, dwell on setbacks, and rarely offer new ideas or proactive input. Over time, this negativity doesn't just stall progress—it drags the whole team down.

When commitment is lacking at the leadership level, the consequences run even deeper. Managers who don't understand the importance of hiring for attitude and alignment may bring on anyone just to fill a schedule. They overlook red flags in favor of convenience, and the result is high turnover and a culture of inconsistency.

Uncommitted employees tend to quit the moment things get difficult, which is precisely when strong teams are needed most.

Worse still, some managers avoid addressing underperformance because they don't want to deal with the hassle of recruiting and training replacements. Keeping the wrong people just to keep bodies on the floor is a costly mistake. One disengaged employee can erode morale and create a toxic atmosphere for the rest of the team. When someone clearly isn't aligned with the company's mission and refuses to meet basic expectations, they need to be let go before the damage spreads.

Implementing Commitment as a Core Value

Building a culture of commitment isn't easy, especially if you're working with a team that includes disengaged or unmotivated people. A strong work ethic is often tied to deeper qualities like integrity and personal responsibility, which can be difficult to instill from scratch. But while you can't force someone to care, you can create the conditions where commitment is encouraged, expected, and rewarded. Here are some practical ways business leaders can cultivate and sustain commitment in their teams:

Model commitment in your own role.

One of the most powerful tools for building a committed team is your own example. Employees are far more likely to care about their work when they see their leaders showing up with purpose, energy, and consistency, even during tough times. If you cut corners, show up late, or approach challenges with a bad attitude, your team will pick up on that and reflect it back. But when you arrive prepared, stay positive, follow through, and give your best effort—even on tough days—you set a standard your team can see and feel.

If you want commitment from your team, show them what it looks like: Arrive on time, greet people with a smile, approach tasks with a solutions-oriented mindset, and maintain high standards in your own work. When leaders stay focused, positive, and dependable, it inspires their team to do the same.

Hire passionate, motivated people.

A strong culture of commitment starts with hiring the right people. Many of the challenges around employee disengagement can be avoided by being more intentional during the hiring process. Don't just look at technical qualifications. Look for signs of genuine motivation and alignment with your values. Ask questions that reveal character and notice how they answer. Does this person work well in teams? Do they take ownership of problems? Are they adaptable? Do they show curiosity and a desire to grow? Are they in it for the long haul or likely to quit when things get hard? How have they handled tough situations at work in the past? Why are they interested in the type of work you're offering? Why do they want to work for *you* rather than some other company?

People who are internally driven will show up with energy, push through challenges, and elevate those around them. You can teach policies and procedures, but you can't teach drive. Always hire for attitude first. The rest can be taken care of later. This creates a workforce where commitment is the norm, not the exception.

Communicate in ways that make committing easy.

If you want employees to commit to your mission, you need to make that mission clear and consistent. Too many businesses fail to reinforce their values in a way that sticks. When messaging shifts frequently or expectations feel unclear, employees lose direction and motivation. Getting their buy-in is nonnegotiable. Core values should be stable guideposts, not moving targets. You can adapt strategies and tweak details as your business evolves, but the underlying principles should stay the same. Keep the mission top of mind by repeating it often in training, in meetings, and in everyday conversations. When your team hears and sees the mission regularly, they're more likely to believe in it and act on it.

Provide employees with great perks.

People are more likely to stay committed to a company that shows commitment to them. Providing thoughtful perks is one way to demonstrate that you value your team not just as workers but as people. Whether it's free meals during lunch breaks, meaningful discounts on services, flexible scheduling, or recognition programs, small gestures can go a long way. When your business becomes a place where employees feel respected, supported, and proud to work, you'll naturally attract and retain more committed individuals. Over time, this creates a flywheel effect. Great perks attract great people, and great people fuel a great workplace culture.

When your team is truly committed to your core values, they'll stay on track without constant supervision. They won't just know the values; they'll believe in them. When employees are aligned with the mission and understand the deeper purpose behind their work, they're more likely to hold themselves accountable. You won't have to micromanage or constantly remind them of what's expected. They'll take initiative, make thoughtful decisions, and act in ways that support the company's goals. This kind of self-driven behavior is a sign that your values have taken root and are guiding actions even when no one's watching. In a committed team, accountability becomes shared, not forced, and that's when real progress happens.

Commitment creates the foundation for a high-performing team that shows up, follows through, and pushes forward even when things get hard. But to truly thrive in a fast-changing world, commitment alone isn't enough. A company also needs curiosity, creativity, and the courage to try new things. That's where innovation comes in. In the next chapter, we'll explore how innovation builds on commitment by challenging teams to think differently, solve problems in new ways, and keep evolving without losing sight of the mission.

Key Takeaways

1. **Commitment is the driving force that sustains all other core values.**

   - It's the promise to stay engaged, adapt, and push forward, especially in times of crisis or uncertainty.

   - Committed employees are purpose-driven, resilient, and solutions-focused; they do what it takes to get the job done.

   - Leadership commitment sets the tone for the entire organization. Without it, even the best vision and strategy will fail.

2. **Lack of commitment erodes performance, morale, and customer experience.**

   - Disengaged team members do the bare minimum, cut corners, and project negativity to coworkers and guests.

   - Uncommitted leaders make poor hiring choices, keep underperformers, and avoid accountability, leading to high turnover and declining standards.

   - Guests notice lapses in service, cleanliness, and safety when commitment is missing—resulting in lost loyalty and revenue.

3. **Leaders can build a culture of commitment through example, hiring, and reinforcement.**

   - Model commitment daily by showing up on time, maintaining high standards, and leading with a positive, solutions-oriented attitude.

   - Hire for attitude and alignment with company values first—skills can be taught, but drive and passion cannot.

   - Reinforce the mission consistently, offer meaningful perks, and create an environment where employees feel respected, trusted, and proud to contribute.

Commitment Self-Assessment Survey

Rate each question from 1 to 5.

(1 = Not true at all / 5 = Consistently true)

1. Do leaders model commitment through consistent behavior, not just through words?

    Rating: _______

2. Do team members follow through on responsibilities without repeated reminders?

    Rating: _______

3. When challenges arise, do people focus on solutions rather than excuses?

    Rating: _______

4. Do employees remain engaged and professional even when work is stressful or repetitive?

    Rating: _______

5. Is underperformance addressed promptly instead of being tolerated for convenience?

    Rating: _______

6. Do people take pride in outcomes, not just in completing tasks?

    Rating: _______

7. Are chronic complaining, gossip, and disengagement discouraged and corrected?

    Rating: _______

8. Do team members understand and believe in what the organization is committed to?

    Rating: _______

9. Do managers stay present and involved during tough periods rather than withdrawing?

   Rating: ______

10. When conditions get difficult, does the team lean in rather than checking out?

   Rating: ______

Scoring & Interpretation

- **40–50 (Strong):** Commitment is embedded and resilient; standards hold under pressure.

- **25–39 (Mixed):** Commitment varies by person or department; momentum is fragile.

- **10–24 (At Risk):** Disengagement is eroding culture; performance will decline without intervention.

Leader Reflection (Answer honestly!)

1. Where have I accepted convenience over commitment?
2. Have I tolerated disengagement to avoid hard conversations?
3. Do people see me staying consistent when results are slow or pressure is high?
4. What negativity have I allowed that is now shaping culture?
5. Would my team describe this culture as resilient—or conditional?

How to Use This Survey

- **Use during stress.** Run it during downturns, transitions, or major change efforts.

- **Audit tolerance.** Identify where disengagement is being excused and why.

- **Link to hiring.** Commitment is partly a people decision; adjust selection and onboarding.

- **Reinforce standards daily.** Commitment grows through small, consistent expectations, not through speeches.

- **Monitor leadership modeling.** The quickest indicator of commitment health is leadership consistency under pressure.

7. Innovation
Finding a Better Way

Innovation is the ability to see change as an opportunity—not a threat.

—Steve Jobs

When I took over Boomers as CEO, I knew turning the business around would require more than just fixing what was broken. We would have to reimagine what was possible. I began walking through each location with fresh eyes, asking myself, "Where are we missing opportunities? How can we create more value for our guests and more revenue for the business?" During one of those walkthroughs, I came across a flat, unremarkable section of concrete. It wasn't serving any purpose. No attractions. No seating. No guests. Just unused space. To me, unused space is wasted potential. I saw an opportunity to transform it into something meaningful that could enhance the guest experience and improve our bottom line. That's when the idea for Boomers Backyard was born. I envisioned a casual, inviting space where families could relax and recharge during their visit. Working with our team, we installed grass, comfortable seating, shaded cabanas, and lush greenery to soften the environment. That once-empty slab of concrete became a revenue-generating hub. Guests began spending more time in the park, and with more time came more spending on snacks, drinks, and extra experiences. The added comfort also improved the overall vibe of the park, making it a place people wanted to return to.

For a business to grow, it must embrace continual change. That's where the core value of innovation comes in. Innovation isn't always about creating something brand-new. More often, it's about seeing existing resources through a different lens and uncovering hidden potential. Truly innovative leaders are always scanning for opportunities to improve, repurpose, or reimagine. They don't wait for perfect conditions or flashy breakthroughs. They work with what they have and make it work smarter. Whether it's underused square footage, overlooked assets, or outdated processes, innovation means unlocking new value from what's already within reach. At the end of the day, growth depends not just on bringing in more guests but on making the most of every guest experience. By using your resources creatively and efficiently, you increase not just revenue but relevance, loyalty, and long-term success.

What Innovation Looks Like in Business

Disney is a machine of innovation. At EPCOT, I watched engineers tweak ride systems overnight, constantly improving flow and guest experience. Even in food service, we innovated. I remember when Sunrise Terrace tried out new fryer baskets to speed throughput. We tested them during rush periods, logged results, and gave feedback. It wasn't about gadgets—it was about always asking, "How can we make this better?"

At the start of the Boomers turnaround, the business model was dated. Games hadn't been refreshed, the menu felt like it came from the 1990s, and parties ran like tired routines. Innovation wasn't luxury; it was survival. We introduced new revenue sources with our VIP areas, Boomers Backyards and Chill Zones; revamped menus with shareable plates and upgraded liquor, beer, and wine; upgraded—or should I say "fixed" —attractions; and tested new pricing models. We also partnered with vendors to bring in trending experiences—without heavy capital spend. Innovation didn't mean inventing the future from scratch. It meant listening to guests, watching competitors, and moving fast. The companies that die aren't usually starved—they're just stale.

At its core, innovation is driven by creativity, the ability to look at what you already have and imagine how it could be better. Innovative business leaders are constantly assessing their environment, identifying gaps, and asking, "How can we make this experience more valuable, more efficient, or more enjoyable?"

This process often starts with observation. Great ideas don't always appear out of thin air. They're often sparked by something seen elsewhere. During the COVID-19 pandemic, for example, I remember walking through a grocery store and noticing the marketing stickers on the floor where the grocery store was trying to sell more green beans and sugar, similar to the circular decals placed on the floor to help customers maintain social distancing. It was a simple, effective visual cue. That sparked an idea: Why not use similar signage at Boomers to sell them pizza, donuts, burgers, specialty drinks, parties, corporate events, etc.? This isn't about copying other businesses. It's about gleaning inspiration and adapting what works to fit your own environment. Guess what? We sold more food and parties from this. Innovation means keeping your eyes open, taking notes, and then applying those insights in ways that align with your unique mission and audience.

Innovative teams are always thinking about how to optimize the guest experience. That might mean reconfiguring layouts, setups, or seating areas to improve flow and comfort. Great hardware stores, for instance, group together matching products like locks and doors in the same aisle. This could also involve integrating more food and beverage opportunities near high-traffic zones to boost revenue. Some airports innovate for a better guest experience by creating spaces where guests can shower, rest, pray, or exercise while waiting for flights. Innovation also means keeping things fresh—rotating in new games, introducing seasonal menu items, and launching themed events that bring people back again and again.

Ultimately, innovation is about making the most of what's in front of you. It's not about waiting for a perfect idea or a big budget. You have to ask, "What could we do differently? What could we try next?" There's no silver bullet, but there are endless opportunities. The most innovative businesses are those that keep evolving, not because they have to, but because they're committed to always finding a better way.

What Happens When Innovation Is Lacking

When innovation is missing from a company's culture, things tend to stay exactly as they are, which is rarely a good thing. These businesses often launch with energy and promise, but once the initial systems are in place, they stop evolving. They settle for "good enough" rather than striving for better. Meanwhile, competitors are adapting, improving their operations, upgrading technology, and staying attuned to changes in customer behavior and cultural expectations. Over time, the gap becomes painfully obvious.

Outdated decor, worn-down equipment, or stale offerings send the message that the business has stopped trying. Guests notice when a space feels neglected or behind the times. It makes them question not only the quality of the experience but even the safety and professionalism of the business. First impressions matter, and an environment that feels frozen in time rarely inspires confidence or enthusiasm. This goes deeper than aesthetics. A lack of innovation often reveals a lack of imagination. These businesses struggle to see new possibilities for using the resources they already have. Empty corners stay empty. Underperforming products never get reimagined. Opportunities for improvement go unnoticed or ignored.

Eventually, customers stop being curious. Without fresh ideas, rotating attractions, or new ways to engage, even loyal guests lose interest. They've seen it all. They've done it all. And without something new to discover, they don't have a reason to come back. Revenue declines. Word of mouth fades. The business becomes irrelevant not because it was bad but because it refused to evolve.

Innovation isn't just about staying trendy. It's about staying alive. In today's fast-moving world, the businesses that succeed are those that keep looking forward and treat every day as an opportunity to try something new, improve something old, and surprise their customers with what's possible.

Implementing Innovation as a Core Value

Innovation doesn't have to be intimidating or a chore. In fact, it can be one of the most exciting and energizing parts of running a business. When innovation becomes a core value, your entire team begins to think more creatively, solve problems more effectively, and look at your business through a lens of possibility. The goal is to build a culture where people are encouraged to ask, "What if we tried this?" and "How could we make this even better?" That kind of thinking is contagious and opens the door to new revenue, happier guests, and a more energized workplace. Here are some practical ways to implement innovation as a company-wide value:

Observe and note great ideas wherever you go.

Some of the best ideas come from simply staying curious as you move through the world. Whether you're visiting another business, walking through a park, or traveling through a new city, be intentional about noticing what catches your attention. Look for elements that spark joy, feel efficient, or surprise you. Maybe it's the layout of a café that creates an inviting atmosphere, the way a theme park guides guests through an experience, or a clever way a retailer uses signage to upsell. Ask yourself, "What's working here and why? Would this approach align with our brand? How could we adapt this idea in a way that feels fresh and authentic to our business?"

You can also gather inspiration from nature, architecture, hospitality, entertainment, and even online platforms. Stay alert to design choices, workflows, or guest experiences that seem intentional and impactful. Take photos. Keep a notebook. Start a shared document or idea board with your team.

Explore ways to differentiate your brand.

Growth depends on continual innovation, and one of the most important questions you can ask yourself is "How can we be different?"

Many people assume innovation requires inventing something completely new, but that's not always true. Often, it's about finding new angles on what already exists. Differentiation can be subtle but powerful.

What are your competitors doing well? What are they doing poorly? Can you take a concept that works elsewhere and tailor it to suit your brand, your property, or your customer base more effectively? Are there underutilized areas on your property that could be transformed to generate more value? Could your layout be more efficient or more welcoming? Could your visual branding, menu, or guest flow feel more intentional? The key is to look at your business with fresh eyes over and over again. The more you challenge yourself to think creatively about what you already have, the more you'll uncover new ways to stand out from the crowd. Innovation through differentiation is what turns "just another business" into a destination.

Figure out what's possible.

One of the biggest roadblocks to innovation is assuming something can't be done before you've truly explored it. Too often, great ideas are abandoned before they have a chance to develop, simply because someone thinks, "That's probably too expensive" or "We've never done that before." This kind of mindset leaves the door wide open for your competitors to take the risks you avoided and reap the rewards you missed.

Instead of shutting an idea down, start by asking the right questions:

Can we do this?

What would it take?

What would it cost, and what kind of return could we expect?

Do we have the right people, or do we need to bring in outside expertise?

Does our team have the capacity and skill set to execute this effectively?

Even if the answer isn't immediately clear, you won't know what's truly possible until you take a closer look. Sometimes an idea that feels out of reach just needs smarter budgeting, a phased rollout, or a creative workaround. Innovation isn't always about big investments. It's about resourcefulness, problem-solving, and bold thinking.

Once you've identified what's possible and confirmed that the idea aligns with your budget and business goals, the next step is simple: Make a plan and act on it.

Get guests to spend more time (and money) at your business.

The longer guests stay at your business, the more likely they are to spend. That's where smart innovation can have a major impact. The key is to create an environment where people want to linger. That means going beyond the basics and offering food, beverages, seating, and other amenities that make the experience more enjoyable. Ask yourself questions like these:

Would it make sense to serve alcohol in our space?

Could an alcohol license eventually pay for itself through increased sales?

Are there underutilized areas where we could add value with shaded seating or kid-friendly play zones?

What types of live performances or seasonal events could draw in crowds and give guests a reason to come back?

Can our brand offer adults-only cruises, flights, or areas so customers without kids will choose us over our competitors?

You should also consider how to keep the energy up and the spending going inside your venue. Can you upgrade your prizes to create a stronger incentive for guests to keep playing your games? Are there ways to bundle experiences or offer promotions that encourage people to explore more of your offerings? If your business lacks retail offerings, could you build a store or several? Restaurant chain Cracker Barrel derives 20 to 30 percent of its profits from retail alone—a lesson all eateries can learn from.

Ultimately, this isn't just about upselling. It's about enriching the guest experience. The more time people spend on-site enjoying themselves, the more likely they are to open their wallets. Innovation in this context is about reimagining the customer journey from start to finish, making every moment more valuable for both the guest and the business.

Rethink layout and sight lines.

While working at Applebee's, I noticed a small but powerful design decision that had a big impact on the guest experience: The bar was sunken into the center of the space. This clever innovation improved visibility across the entire restaurant. Guests could see what was happening around them, and staff could move more efficiently with better awareness of the dining floor. That one choice improved aesthetics while enhancing flow, communication, and comfort.

This inspired me to apply the same principle to Boomers Parks. I began evaluating the park not just from a functional perspective but from the eyes of the guest. Were our spaces easy to navigate? Could people see where they wanted to go, or were we unintentionally creating confusion and visual clutter? In many areas, overgrown foliage and physical obstructions were blocking sight lines, making it hard for guests to find food stands, restrooms, or key attractions. We made it a priority to clean up and open up those spaces. The result? Guests had clearer views across the park, making them more likely to explore, make purchases, and stay longer because they weren't wasting time looking for what they needed.

If you're marketing to the wrong demographic, change your approach.

Innovation doesn't just apply to what happens inside your business. It also applies to who you're trying to reach and how you're reaching them. If your business isn't as profitable as it should be, part of the problem may be your target demographic. You might be offering the right services but promoting them to the wrong audience. Ask yourself the following questions:

Are we attracting the type of guests who are willing—and able—to spend money here?

Could a few strategic upgrades justify raising prices and appealing to a higher-income demographic?

Are our marketing materials speaking the language, values, or interests of the audience we actually want to attract?

Sometimes, making your business more profitable means positioning it differently. This could involve refreshing your branding, improving the aesthetics of your space, or introducing premium experiences that align with a more affluent or experience-focused customer base. It could also mean reassessing your advertising platforms to ensure you're reaching the right people through social media, local partnerships, and community events.

Don't be afraid to pivot. One of the most powerful forms of innovation is the willingness to course-correct. When you align your offerings with the right audience and speak to their needs, interests, and values, you not only attract customers who are a better fit but also set your business up for longer-term sustainability and success.

Update your technology to fit modern standards.

Innovation and technology go hand in hand. In today's business environment, outdated tech signals to guests that your business isn't keeping up. By embracing new tools and systems, you can enhance both the efficiency of your operations and the quality of your guest experience. Start by looking at the basics. Instead of static, one-size-fits-all signage, could you use digital screens that rotate content throughout the day? This step can help with things like advertising events, promoting food specials, or sharing wait times. These small upgrades can make your business feel more dynamic and engaging.

You can also explore how technology can streamline operations. Is there operations software that can help with scheduling, inventory management, or maintenance tracking? Could a mobile app allow guests to view menus from their phone? Are you using customer data to personalize experiences, offer promotions, or reward loyalty?

For more experiential innovation, consider bigger investments like virtual reality attractions, interactive kiosks, or even robotics for service or entertainment purposes. These kinds of upgrades modernize your offering, set your brand apart, and create memorable experiences that drive return visits. Ultimately, staying current with technology is about creating smoother processes, faster service, and a more exciting environment that meets the expectations of today's guests.

There's no limit to how creative you can get when it comes to innovation. Whether it's a bold new attraction, a subtle change in layout, or a reimagined way of using your existing resources, every improvement adds momentum. The most successful businesses evolve, adapt, and reinvent themselves over time. By making thoughtful changes consistently—not just when things break or profits dip—you stay ahead of the curve, surprise your guests, and inspire your team. Innovation is a mindset, and when it becomes part of your culture, there's no end to what your business can achieve.

The most effective innovations are the ones that not only delight your guests but also strengthen your bottom line. In the next chapter, we'll explore how to make profitability a core value so your business isn't just exciting but also sustainable.

Key Takeaways

1. **Innovation is about reimagining what you already have.**

   - It's not always about inventing something brand-new—often, it's finding new ways to use underutilized space, assets, or processes to create value.

   - Innovative leaders look with fresh eyes, spot opportunities others overlook, and adapt ideas from anywhere to fit their brand and audience.

   - The goal is continual improvement that enhances the guest experience, drives revenue, and keeps the business relevant.

2. **Without innovation, businesses stagnate and lose relevance.**

   - Companies that stop evolving send the message that they've stopped trying, leading to outdated offerings, declining customer interest, and loss of loyalty.

   - Competitors who adapt to changing guest needs, technology, and cultural trends will quickly pull ahead.

   - Stale experiences erode curiosity and repeat visits, even if the original concept was strong.

3. **Innovation can be systematic and strategic.**

   - Build a culture where the team constantly asks, "What could we try next?" and evaluates ideas based on feasibility, ROI, and brand fit.

   - Differentiate from competitors through layout improvements, upgraded amenities, technology updates, targeted marketing, and experiences that encourage guests to stay longer.

   - Embrace flexibility—pivoting demographics, adding seasonal events, or updating tech—so the business stays fresh, engaging, and profitable.

Innovation Self-Assessment Survey

Rate each question from 1 to 5.

(1 = Not true at all / 5 = Consistently true)

1. Do leaders regularly walk the business with fresh eyes, looking for untapped potential?

   Rating: _______

2. Is questioning "how it's always been done" encouraged rather than dismissed?

   Rating: _______

3. Are new ideas evaluated thoughtfully rather than shut down prematurely?

   Rating: _______

4. Does guest behavior and feedback directly influence improvements?

   Rating: _______

5. Are small, low-risk tests used before making larger commitments?

   Rating: _______

6. Are offerings, environments, or processes refreshed proactively rather than only after decline?

   Rating: _______

7. Does innovation focus on both the guest experience and financial performance?

   Rating: _______

8. Do teams borrow ideas from other industries and adapt them effectively?

   Rating: _______

9. Does leadership allocate time and resources for experimentation and improvement?

Rating: _______

10. Does the organization view change as an opportunity rather than as a disruption or threat?

Rating: _______

Scoring & Interpretation

- **40–50 (Strong):** Innovation is embedded; the organization stays fresh and competitive.

- **25–39 (Mixed):** Innovation is reactive; improvements happen under pressure rather than by design.

- **10–24 (At Risk):** Stagnation is present; relevance and growth are threatened.

Leader Reflection (Answer honestly!)

1. Where are we tolerating "good enough" that guests have already outgrown?

2. Do we default to "too risky" before exploring small-test options?

3. When was the last time we tested something new with minimal cost and clear measurement?

4. Are we improving faster than the market—or falling behind?

5. Do leaders create space for innovation or crowd it out with urgency?

How to Use This Survey

- **Use during planning cycles.** Run it before budget allocation and strategic planning.

- **Create a pilot pipeline.** Translate low scores into two or three pilots with clear ownership and timelines.

- **Measure what matters.** Track guest response, operational impact, and financial results.

- **Avoid "innovation theater."** Focus on improvements that change outcomes, not just ideas.

- **Revisit semiannually.** Innovation needs cadence; otherwise, it becomes reactive.

8. Profitability
The Engine That Sustains Everything

Profit is not the explanation, cause, or rationale of business behavior and business decisions, but the test of their validity.

—Peter Drucker

Back in chapter one, I shared a glimpse of my dad's journey as a businessman. He worked incredibly hard when I was a kid but never ended up getting particularly wealthy. He was too gracious, always supporting others financially when they needed it, and people took advantage of that kindness. Even with his work ethic, he still had to worry constantly about money as a business owner. Watching him worry taught me early on how much profits matter. Many business owners and leaders shy away from financial reports or leave the numbers to someone else because they feel overwhelmed or uninterested. But the truth is you can't afford to look away. A business without profit is essentially on borrowed time. No matter how noble the mission or how hard the team works, if the business isn't financially healthy, it all slips away eventually.

A business can't sustain itself unless it's consistently profitable. For this reason, profitability must be a core value embedded into how your company operates. On your turf, you can charge whatever you want for your products and services, but you must master a winning strategy for managing and multiplying that income. Your ideal customer demographic will prioritize the experience, outcome, and value you deliver. Price only becomes a major concern if they don't get the experience they were promised.

What Profitability Looks Like in Business

At Disney Finance, I discovered that every magical guest smile had a cost. Fireworks weren't free; neither were cast uniforms nor the armies of custodial staff who kept EPCOT spotless. Profitability wasn't greed—it was fuel. Without it, the magic doesn't last. That shaped my thinking forever: You can love the mission, but you must fund the mission.

Boomers was bleeding when I arrived. Everyone wanted to talk about "vision" and "guest experience." Those mattered, but if we didn't fix profitability, none of it would survive. We attacked the cost of goods sold, renegotiated leases, reset labor models, and eliminated underperforming programs. It wasn't glamorous work—but month by month, the red shrank and eventually flipped to black. Profitability didn't replace fun—it protected it. Only a profitable company can reinvest in guests, people, and growth.

Profitable businesses are key drivers of innovation because they have the security and flexibility to take financial risks. When a company is financially healthy, it has the freedom to take smart risks, try new ideas, and grow strategically. Leaders who know their numbers inside and out can make bold moves with confidence, whether that means opening new locations, expanding the team, offering better employee benefits, or giving back to their communities. When profits are strong and steady, opportunities that once felt out of reach suddenly become possible.

Profitability isn't just a leadership concern. It thrives when it becomes a shared value across the entire organization. When managers and staff embrace profitability as part of the company culture, they see beyond their day-to-day tasks. They understand why prices are set a certain way, who the target customer is, and how their individual choices affect the bottom line. Instead of viewing profits as something selfish or greedy, they recognize that profitability is what allows the business to grow, support its team, serve its customers better, and make a broader impact. They understand that when the business succeeds, everyone in its orbit does too.

What Happens When Profitability Is Lacking

A lack of profitability signals the slow decline of a business. When revenue is consistently falling, and customers stop showing up, it's a red flag that something deeper is wrong. Often, the issue stems from a company culture that doesn't prioritize profitability or educate staff on its importance. Waste becomes common. Food gets tossed, portions are oversized, and resources are misused. Employees don't see the connection between these small daily actions and the company's financial health. As a result, they may resist price increases, ignore sales targets, and feel disconnected from the broader goals of the business. In some cases, theft becomes a problem—whether it's cash disappearing from the register or supplies from the stockroom—further draining already thin margins.

On the leadership side, poor financial discipline only makes things worse. Some owners avoid financial reports altogether, outsourcing everything to bookkeepers without understanding what the numbers are actually telling them. They may spend impulsively, signing leases they can't sustain, hiring too aggressively, or making high-ticket purchases without a plan. There's a dangerous assumption that things will somehow work out, but without accountability and clarity around profitability, the consequences are real: layoffs, closures, and in the worst cases, bankruptcy. When profitability is missing, it's only a matter of time before everything collapses.

Implementing Profitability as a Core Value

Profitability is more about mindset than the numbers themselves. Successful business leaders understand that the real game is turning what you have into more. It's about being intentional with every part of the operation. How can you increase revenue per customer? How can every square foot of your space work harder for the business? They also know profitability isn't a solo effort but a team sport. No product sells itself. It takes people who care, provide excellent service, and understand the role they play in creating value. When the whole team is aligned around profitability, the impact is exponential. Here are some practical ways to move your business out of the red and into the black:

Boost the amount of money you make per guest.

Chasing volume by keeping prices low and trying to pack the business often leads to more stress than success. Instead of relying on foot traffic alone, focus on increasing the value of each individual customer. The more effective strategy, especially in the long run, is often to raise your prices and deliver a premium experience that justifies that cost. Don't be afraid to target a more affluent customer demographic so you can charge more. You're the one setting the prices and defining the value. After you raise prices, look for ways to encourage guests to stay longer and spend more while they're with you. Can they enjoy a meal and a drink on-site? Do you offer comfortable places to relax when they need a break? Are there spaces for socializing or browsing products? The longer they stay, the more opportunities you have to drive revenue. If your guests feel like they get great value for their money, they won't resent paying a higher price.

Visit your branch locations and talk to the managers.

If you work at the corporate level, make it a priority to regularly visit your company's branch locations. There's no substitute for seeing things firsthand. Financial problems, even bankruptcy, often take root when local managers aren't following through on key responsibilities or when standards begin to slip unnoticed. Make sure budgets are being used appropriately and resources are being managed wisely. Sit down with your managers, review their numbers, and have open, honest conversations about what's working and what's not. Transparency and collaboration are key. You're on the same team, working toward the same goals. The more aligned you are, the stronger the entire business becomes.

Know what it costs to make what you sell.

In the food and beverage world, your product is consumed and replaced every single day. That makes it essential to understand your product mix and what it really costs to produce each item. What's your profit margin per plate? Are you clear on the cost breakdown of every dish you serve? As a rule of thumb, your cost-to-profit margin should be 20 percent or less. If it's higher, there's a good chance you're losing money to things like theft, portion creep, or excessive food waste. The goal is to keep your theoretical costs and actual costs as close as possible. Sometimes, small changes make a big difference. Reducing portion sizes—even something as simple as serving fewer fries—can add up to tens or even hundreds of thousands of dollars in recovered profit over time. Don't accept high food costs as inevitable. Get strategic, tighten your operations, and make every plate count.

Experiment with your prices.

Pricing isn't a one-time decision. It's something you should constantly test and refine. A good starting point is to multiply your cost by five. Then consider what your target customer is likely willing to pay based on the value you're delivering. Do some research, test different price points, and see what resonates. Set your prices at a level your ideal customer finds acceptable, then raise them gradually over time to keep pace with inflation and rising costs. If you're truly offering something of value, chances are you can charge more than you initially think. Don't be afraid to push your pricing, as long as the experience you're providing backs it up.

Figure out what your profits should be.

How much profit should your business actually be making? The answer depends on your industry and business model. For example, nonprofits might operate comfortably with a 10 percent profit margin. That's perfectly acceptable for their mission-driven goals. But if you're running a corporation, especially one with investors or shareholders, your profit targets will need to be significantly higher to meet expectations and sustain growth. Take time to research typical profit margins in your sector. Look at industry reports, consult with experts, and compare your numbers to those of businesses similar to yours. The goal is to understand what's standard and then work toward hitting or exceeding that target. A healthy profit is essential to keeping your business viable and competitive.

Bundle offerings into packages.

One of the simplest ways to increase perceived value and justify higher prices is by bundling your offerings into curated packages. When guests can experience multiple aspects of your business in one purchase, it feels like they're getting more for their money. For example, instead of selling just a single round of mini golf, you might offer a package that includes food and drinks. This not only enhances the overall experience but also encourages customers to spend more than they would on a single item or service. Strategic bundling boosts revenue while delivering a more memorable and convenient experience for your guests.

Charge premium prices for group bookings.

If your business hosts events like birthday parties, weddings, or group celebrations, you have a prime opportunity to boost profitability and visibility at the same time. Large gatherings bring in more revenue at once while introducing your business to dozens of potential future customers. Don't be shy about charging premium prices for group bookings. Just be sure to clearly communicate the value they're getting in return. Exceptional service, seamless coordination, and a memorable experience go a long way with groups. Go above and beyond to impress every guest so when it's their turn to celebrate, your business is top of mind. Consider giving out branded items like T-shirts or goody bags that guests can take home. Not only does it enhance the experience, but it also empowers them to advertise your company long after the party ends.

Explain to your team how the finances work.

When the timing is right, take the opportunity to clearly explain to your team how the business's finances work. Many employees simply don't have insight into what it takes to keep a business profitable, and that lack of understanding can lead to disconnect or even mistrust.

Break it down for them on all levels. Why is profitability a core value? What keeps the business in the black, and what happens when it's not? How do everyday decisions around waste, service quality, upselling, or efficiency directly impact the company's bottom line? Most importantly, how can your team contribute to improving profits, and why should it matter to them? Don't assume your employees naturally value profitability the way you do. Some may come from backgrounds where money was seen in a negative light. They may assume anyone focused on profit—especially from corporate or leadership—cares more about money than people. That perception can be damaging unless you address it head-on.

Take time to connect, communicate, and show them that profitability isn't about greed. It's about sustainability, growth, and creating a workplace where everyone can thrive. When your team understands the bigger picture and feels like they're part of it, they're far more likely to get behind your goals and help drive success.

The more profitable your business is, the more freedom you have to take bold, innovative risks. Profit gives you the power to grow, experiment, and invest in the future. This isn't just up to leadership; every team member plays a role. When everyone works together to make small, smart changes that boost profitability, the results compound. That momentum creates room for even bigger moves ahead.

Once you've stabilized your finances and created systems that generate consistent profit, you unlock the ability to grow through collaboration. That's where strategic partnerships come in. In the next chapter, we'll explore how to identify, build, and nurture strategic relationships that move your business forward and solidify your influence in your community.

Key Takeaways

1. **Profitability is essential for sustainability and growth.**

   - Without consistent profit, even mission-driven or hard-working businesses eventually fail.

   - Profit enables innovation, strategic risk-taking, expansion, and better support for both customers and employees.

   - Profitability should be embraced as a shared core value across the organization—not just a leadership concern—so every team member understands their role in financial health.

2. **Lack of profitability signals deeper cultural and operational problems.**

   - Waste, theft, oversized portions, and poor resource management erode margins when employees don't connect their actions to the bottom line.

   - Leaders who ignore financial reports, overspend, or avoid discipline create instability that can lead to layoffs, closures, or bankruptcy.

   - A culture that avoids talking about profit breeds resistance to necessary price changes and misses opportunities to improve revenue.

3. **Profitability can be built through strategic pricing, efficiency, and team alignment.**

   - Increase revenue per guest by offering premium experiences, bundling, and group pricing and by encouraging longer visits.

   - Know your cost structure, monitor margins closely, and adjust pricing through testing and gradual increases to maintain healthy profits.

   - Educate the team on how the business makes money, connect profitability to shared success, and empower staff to make small daily decisions that drive the numbers upward.

Profitability Self-Assessment Survey

Rate each question from 1 to 5.

(1 = Not true at all / 5 = Consistently true)

1. Do leaders understand the key financial drivers of the business?

   Rating: _______

2. Do managers know their numbers and understand variances without guessing?

   Rating: _______

3. Does pricing reflect delivered value rather than fear of guest reaction?

   Rating: _______

4. Is revenue per guest—not just traffic or volume—actively prioritized?

   Rating: _______

5. Are costs monitored and addressed proactively rather than after losses appear?

   Rating: _______

6. Are waste, theft, and inefficiency taken seriously and corrected quickly?

   Rating: _______

7. Are underperforming programs or assets improved or eliminated when necessary?

   Rating: _______

8. Are financial decisions made intentionally rather than impulsively or emotionally?

   Rating: _______

9. Do team members understand how daily actions impact profitability?

   Rating: _______

10. Is profitability discussed openly as a requirement for sustainability rather than avoided?

   Rating: _______

Scoring & Interpretation

- **40–50 (Strong):** Financial discipline is embedded; the business can reinvest and grow.

- **25–39 (Mixed):** Profit focus is inconsistent; margins are vulnerable.

- **10–24 (At Risk):** Profitability is threatened; sustainability is at risk.

Leader Reflection (Answer honestly!)

1. Where am I avoiding the numbers because they feel uncomfortable?
2. Are we pricing based on value or fear?
3. Are we increasing revenue per guest or just working harder for less?
4. Do managers truly own the profit-and-loss drivers—or only explain outcomes?
5. What cost or revenue leak have we accepted as "normal" that shouldn't be?

How to Use This Survey

- **Use before expansion.** Run it before new units, remodels, hiring spikes, or capex commitments.

- **Review with owners of drivers.** Assign each low area to a leader who controls that lever.

- **Translate into habits.** Create routines: weekly labor reviews, monthly cost audits, pricing reviews, waste controls.

- **Educate teams.** Teach employees how their actions connect to profit and sustainability.

- **Revisit quarterly.** Margin erosion is gradual; quarterly reviews prevent drift.

9. Partnership
Winning With, Not Against, Others

Success is best when it's shared.

—Howard Schultz

During my time working for the former chairman and CEO at Applebee's International, I learned the value of strategic partnerships. The managers there didn't just focus on running a restaurant but on building relationships as well. They knew the city's mayor by name. They had strong ties with the local police and fire departments. When these groups finished their shifts or wanted to celebrate a special occasion, Applebee's was their go-to spot. Every year, they came back for holiday parties, anniversaries, networking events, and team dinners. These recurring events became a reliable source of income and community visibility. Because of those partnerships, the restaurant became a hub for the neighborhood. People talked about it, recommended it, and kept coming back. That experience taught me that when you invest in the right relationships, they can take your business further than marketing ever could.

Strategic partnerships are intentional, long-term collaborations between two or more organizations that work together to achieve shared goals. All businesses that bring on partnership as a core value, no matter their size or industry, can benefit from strategic partnerships that open up new streams of income and increase visibility. The right partnership can help you reach new audiences, enhance your brand, and create experiences that keep customers coming back. What kinds of partnerships make the most sense for your business? Who shares your audience, values, or goals? When you identify the right allies and build mutually beneficial relationships, you create momentum that's hard to achieve alone.

What Partnership Looks Like in Business

My father's businesses were built on partnerships. He traded labor with friends, swapped services with suppliers, and treated customers like neighbors. At EPCOT, partnership looked like teamwork under fire—servers, cooks, and cashiers backing each other up during insane lunch rushes. If one person collapsed, the whole line did. That forged my instinct: *Partnership multiplies performance.* At Boomers, we partnered with vendors to secure better deals, with landlords to reset terms, and with employees to cocreate solutions. I made it clear: I wasn't parachuting in as the hero. I was linking arms. When people feel like partners instead of pawns, they rise higher. And they did.

Strategic partnerships can be a powerful way for businesses to grow, helping them reach new audiences, reduce costs, access specialized expertise, build customer loyalty, and boost brand credibility. When partnership is embraced as a core value, business leaders are always on the lookout for ways to collaborate with like-minded organizations, especially within their local communities.

One well-known example is the partnership between Nike and Apple. Apple integrated Nike's fitness branding into its products, most notably the Apple Watch. The collaboration gave Apple greater credibility in the fitness space while providing Nike with innovative tools to deepen customer engagement. Both brands stayed true to their identities while gaining access to each other's strengths, providing a perfect example of a mutually beneficial relationship.

At the local level, strategic partnerships can look a little different but be just as effective. Smart organizations often cohost events, offer exclusive discounts to each other's customers or employees, and collaborate on giveaways or raffles. For example, at a theme park where I once worked, we partnered with a local car dealership. The dealership paid to display one of their vehicles on-site at the park and offered guests a chance to win a free car. People would take pictures with it, interact with the brand, and learn more about the car, while our park earned passive revenue from the sponsorship.

The best partnerships go beyond one-time promotions. They're ongoing relationships with companies that have strong marketing programs and active audiences. Great partners promote each other through social media, websites, and even commercials, keeping both brands top of mind within each other's communities. Done right, strategic partnerships create long-term momentum through shared exposure, shared trust, and shared success.

What Happens When Partnership Is Lacking

A business without partnerships is like a remote island in the middle of the ocean. It may occasionally attract passersby who stumble across it, but it lacks steady, reliable traffic and connection to the broader network of commerce. Without strategic partnerships, an organization stands alone, disconnected from the community and cut off from mutually beneficial relationships that could strengthen its sales, marketing, and visibility.

When businesses don't build partnerships, they miss valuable opportunities for collaboration, exposure, and growth. There's no one out there promoting them, inviting them to events, or sharing their name with new audiences. Instead of being a go-to destination for group gatherings, special events, or cross-promotions, they're passed over in favor of more connected, visible alternatives.

Without those ties, businesses struggle to stay top of mind. Other organizations don't talk about them. Guests don't think to visit. And the broader community has little incentive to rally around them. Ultimately, without partnerships, a business limits not only its reach but also its potential for long-term success and relevance.

Implementing Partnership as a Core Value

When partnership is embraced as a core value, it shifts the mindset of your leadership team. Managers and other decision-makers begin to actively look for opportunities to collaborate rather than trying to do everything in isolation. With the right guidance, they can identify and build relationships with partners that not only align with your brand but also bring real value through increased revenue, exposure, or community engagement. Strategic partnerships aren't just about convenience but also intentional alignment. The right partnerships can amplify your efforts and open up new possibilities for growth. Here are some practical tips for identifying and forming meaningful strategic partnerships:

Identify the right partners for your business.

Not every partnership is a good fit. Choosing the right collaborators starts with understanding your audience. The most effective partnerships align with your brand, your customer base, and your business goals. For example, it wouldn't make much sense for a winery to partner with organizations that market to teenagers. A partnership with an upscale art gallery or resort might be a perfect match, however, because they share the same target demographic. Think about who your customers are. Why do they come to your business? What do they care about, and what other brands or experiences do they already engage with? The best partnerships are ones that enhance the experience for your guests while also delivering value to the partner. Look for alignment not just in audience but in energy, tone, and values. A great partnership should feel like a natural extension of your brand and a win-win for everyone involved.

Communicate the benefits of partnering with you.

Any partner you collaborate with will want to know what's in it for them. To build a strong foundation, you need to clearly articulate the value your business brings to the table. How will partnering with you support their goals, expand their reach, or positively impact their bottom line? Maybe you attract a specific audience they want to reach. Maybe you can offer them consistent event traffic, cobranded exposure, or passive advertising opportunities. Whatever it is, define the value in clear, tangible terms.

Before diving into the details of a potential partnership, make sure the benefits are well understood and that they go both ways. A strong partnership is always a win-win built on aligned goals and shared success. When you can communicate your value with confidence, you're much more likely to attract partners who are equally committed to making the collaboration work.

Ask if partners are willing to pay to advertise at your locations.

One simple but effective way to generate passive income is by offering your strategic partners the opportunity to advertise at your business. This creates a valuable marketing channel for them and an easy revenue stream for you. The advertising doesn't have to be flashy or intrusive. In fact, subtlety often works better. A small, well-designed plaque, sign, or branded display can catch guests' attention without disrupting the atmosphere. Done tastefully, it can even add to the professional look and feel of your space. If you're already partnering with businesses that align with your brand and audience, paid in-location advertising is a natural next step and a smart way to boost profits with minimal effort in what would be considered sponsorships.

Become the go-to destination for your partners' events.

Your strategic partners are constantly looking for venues to host their gatherings, which might include school functions, corporate team-building activities, networking mixers, chamber of commerce events, retirement celebrations, or annual holiday parties. These events are happening year-round, and if you position your business as a welcoming, reliable host, you can become their go-to destination.

Offer small but meaningful perks to make their experience special. That might include access to a private room, light hospitality support, or a few complimentary drinks. These gestures may seem minor to you, but to your partners, they create a sense of appreciation and VIP treatment. In return, they're likely to support your business by purchasing food, drinks, or services during and after the event. The goal is to treat your partners so well and create such positive, memorable experiences that they don't even consider going anywhere else. When you become their trusted go-to spot, you're not just gaining one-time revenue but building long-term loyalty and word-of-mouth visibility throughout their networks.

Sell your partners' products at your events.

Events are prime opportunities to strengthen partnerships while boosting revenue and visibility. If you're hosting a concert, a festival, a tournament, or even a themed night at your business, consider cosponsoring the event with one of your partners. A well-attended event gives both of you a chance to shine. For example, if your partner is a soft drink brand, you could feature their product with custom signage, branded booths, or exclusive promotions. You could even host a charity raffle or giveaway featuring a partner's product, like a free airline ticket or vacation package, which adds excitement while promoting their brand.

The idea is to create shared momentum. How can you spotlight your partner's products during your events? And, just as importantly, how can they feature *your* products or services at theirs? Strategic cross-promotion extends your reach, adds value for customers, and strengthens the relationship between both businesses.

Focus on what's popular locally.

One of the most effective ways to build meaningful partnerships is to align with what matters most in your local community. Look around. What defines the area you serve? If you're near a military base, for example, consider partnering with organizations that support service members and their families. If your region has a strong Latino population, connect with businesses and groups that serve and celebrate that community. When you form partnerships that reflect the interests, identities, and values of your neighbors, your business becomes more than just a place to visit. You become part of the community's fabric. People take notice when you support the groups they care about. They're more likely to return the favor by supporting your business in return. The more locally relevant your partnerships are, the more likely your business is to stay top of mind and be seen as a trusted, community-centered brand.

Implementing a core value around strategic partnerships does more than boost your bottom line. It helps embed your business into the heart of the community. By forming thoughtful collaborations, you create lasting connections that drive repeat visits, word-of-mouth referrals, and shared success. With the right partnerships in place, your business can become a trusted, go-to destination for local organizations, events, and everyday experiences.

When you team up with the right people and organizations, you can create real, positive impact in your community. This feeds into our final core value: social responsibility. In the next chapter, we'll explore how giving back and doing the right thing can strengthen your brand, motivate your team, and keep your business rooted in purpose.

Key Takeaways

1. **Strategic partnerships multiply reach, revenue, and reputation.**

   - The right collaborations open access to new audiences, enhance credibility, and generate recurring income streams that marketing alone can't achieve.

   - Partnerships work best when values, audiences, and goals are aligned—creating a win-win that benefits both sides over the long term.

   - Local partnerships, like relationships with civic groups, schools, or community organizations, can turn a business into a trusted neighborhood hub.

2. **A lack of partnerships limits growth and community connection.**

   - Without partners promoting and collaborating with you, your business is isolated, less visible, and more likely to be passed over for connected competitors.

   - Missed opportunities for copromotion, events, and cross-selling mean slower growth and less brand recognition.

   - Partnerships keep your brand top of mind through ongoing exposure, referrals, and shared community presence.

3. **Successful partnerships are intentional, mutually beneficial, and actively nurtured.**

   - Identify partners whose audience overlaps with yours and whose brand energy complements your own.

   - Clearly communicate the benefits you bring—whether it's access to your customers, event hosting, or paid on-site advertising opportunities.

   - Deepen relationships through cohosted events, selling partner products, offering VIP treatment for partner gatherings, and aligning with what's popular locally to strengthen community ties.

Partnership Self-Assessment Survey

Rate each question from 1 to 5.

(1 = Not true at all / 5 = Consistently true)

1. Does the business actively pursue partnerships aligned with its brand, audience, and values?

    Rating: ______

2. Are partnerships approached with a long-term mindset rather than with one-off promotions?

    Rating: ______

3. Are partnerships structured to deliver clear value to both parties?

    Rating: ______

4. Does the organization collaborate with local groups that matter to the community?

    Rating: ______

5. Do partnerships drive recurring events, group business, or repeat traffic?

    Rating: ______

6. Are partners encouraged and enabled to promote the business through their channels?

    Rating: ______

7. Does the business offer partners meaningful visibility or engagement opportunities?

    Rating: ______

8. Do leaders invest time in maintaining relationships after agreements are signed?

    Rating: ______

9. Are partnership results measured (revenue, exposure, loyalty, referrals)?

   Rating: _______

10. Is the business viewed by partners as a trusted, reliable destination?

   Rating: _______

Scoring & Interpretation

- **40–50 (Strong):** Partnerships are active and compounding; growth is accelerated through alignment.

- **25–39 (Mixed):** Partnerships exist but are inconsistent or underleveraged.

- **10–24 (At Risk):** The business operates in isolation; growth opportunities are being missed.

Leader Reflection (Answer honestly!)

1. Who actively advocates for us when we are not in the room?
2. Are our partnerships truly mutual or mostly transactional?
3. Do we nurture relationships after the deal or just move on to the next one?
4. What partnership category are we ignoring (schools, corporate, nonprofits, tourism, sports, etc.)?
5. If our business disappeared, which partners would feel the loss—and why?

How to Use This Survey

- **Use during marketing planning.** Partnership is a strategic lever—plan it; don't improvise it.

- **Build a partner pipeline.** Create a target list and assign ownership for outreach and maintenance.

- **Measure outcomes.** Track referrals, group sales, event attendance, and promotional reach.

- **Strengthen repeatability.** Convert one-off partnerships into recurring events or seasonal programs.

- **Revisit semiannually.** Partnerships drift if not nurtured; refresh and recommit regularly.

10. Social Responsibility
Leaving Things Better Than You Found Them

Businesses that put purpose at the heart of their strategy outperform those that don't.

—Paul Polman

When I took over operations at Boomers Parks, I wanted to root each location more deeply in its local community. I believed our parks could be more than entertainment venues. They could be community partners, giving back in meaningful ways. That vision started to take shape in Southern California after a powerful conversation with a woman who used to do catering at one of our parks many years ago. She was a survivor of a violent sexual assault and had since dedicated herself to advocacy work on behalf of others like her. She had connections with local police departments, the California highway patrol, district attorneys, and various civic organizations that she believed might be interested in visiting our parks, not just for fun but for a greater cause. Moved by her story and inspired by her mission, we decided to open two Boomers locations in Southern California twice a year for free for weekend events to benefit crime survivors, and we paid for the labor and expenses. The impact was immediate. The events drew attention, built goodwill, and created community ties that continued to strengthen the Boomers brand.

When your business stands for something bigger than profit, people take notice and show up. Social responsibility, when treated as a core value, goes beyond good ethics. It becomes a powerful differentiator that shapes how your business is remembered. Giving back to your community creates lasting goodwill, strengthens your brand's reputation, and builds deep emotional connections with your guests. Just as importantly, it gives your team a sense of pride and purpose. When people know their work contributes to something meaningful, they feel more motivated, more loyal, and more connected to the mission. Social responsibility is about building a legacy that lasts.

What Social Responsibility Looks Like in Business

At the Spirit of '76, my dad drilled it into us: Keep the place clean, treat neighbors with respect, and remember you represent the family name. Disney reinforced that with scale. Trash wasn't left to "someone else"—everyone picked it up. I saw managers bend down to sweep up popcorn and pick up spilled fries. That modeled a bigger truth: Business is part of the community, not separate from it. Once my team and I had stabilized Boomers during its turnaround, I insisted we give back. We ran free days for underprivileged kids, supported local schools, and opened our doors for charity events. Some questioned the expense. But I'd argue it wasn't expense—it was investment. A business that takes without giving eventually loses not just goodwill but also its soul. Social responsibility anchored our comeback. Families didn't just spend money with us—they felt proud we were in their town.

In businesses where social responsibility is a core value, giving back is part of the everyday culture. These companies get involved in the fabric of their local communities, showing up at chamber of commerce events, city festivals, school functions, and initiatives with police, fire departments, and civic organizations. They build thoughtful partnerships that reflect the values of their community and align with their company's mission. Often, this looks like fundraising drives, donation matching, volunteer events, 5K races, or offers of space and support for local causes. These efforts don't go unnoticed. In a world filled with complex problems, companies that actively work to make a difference stand out, which becomes a competitive edge. People want to support businesses that care.

Over time, these contributions build something deeper than customer loyalty. They create genuine friendships and lasting goodwill. Businesses that show up for their communities are seen not just as service providers but as allies, supporters, and friends. And when people recognize your business as part of something greater, they're more likely to return, refer others, and remain loyal over the long term.

There's also a profound impact inside the business. Employees feel proud to be part of something meaningful. Their work feels like it matters. Instead of just clocking in for a paycheck, they feel like they're helping move the needle on issues that affect real lives. This is especially important for younger generations, who increasingly seek purpose-driven work and want to be part of organizations that reflect their values.

At the end of the day, we all think about what kind of legacy we're leaving behind. Did we make a difference? Did we help someone? Through consistent, values-driven actions, businesses have the chance to be remembered as forces for good. In a world that's hungry for hope and connection, everyone wants to support the helpers.

What Happens When Responsibility Is Lacking

I've seen firsthand the consequences of business leaders overlooking the importance of social responsibility and community relationships. When I began my role as CFO at Applebee's, I quickly learned that the team before me had damaged the company's standing with local city commissioners. While trying to secure a liquor license, they approached the officials with arrogance and entitlement, offending the very people whose support they needed. As a result, the request was denied. When I stepped in, I took a different approach—one built on respect, humility, and a genuine desire to build lasting relationships. I made it a priority to connect with local leaders in a friendly, cooperative way. That shift in tone made all the difference. We not only resolved the immediate issue but also set the foundation for long-term goodwill. It became clear to me that positive community relationships aren't optional. They're often the deciding factor between success and failure.

Inside organizations that neglect social responsibility, you can often feel what's missing. Employees don't see the business as part of something bigger than itself. Managers aren't thinking about local partnerships, community outreach, or how the company's actions affect its neighbors. There's no sense of connection to the surrounding people or causes that matter to them. Instead, the focus stays on internal goals alone. The long-term cost of that disconnect is a weak legacy. Businesses that fail to embrace social responsibility are easily forgotten. They don't build the kind of emotional loyalty that turns customers into advocates or staff into believers. And when they eventually close their doors or change hands, there are few people left in the community who feel invested in remembering or continuing their mission.

That's a missed opportunity. Every business, large or small, has the chance to make a lasting mark. Without genuine investment in the people around you, even the most impressive accomplishments can fade quickly. Relationships, respect, and responsibility are what give your work staying power.

Implementing Responsibility as a Core Value

Making social responsibility a core value starts with expanding the mindset of your entire team. Yes, profit matters, but it shouldn't be the only thing that guides decisions. When your leaders and staff begin thinking beyond the bottom line and considering how their work can contribute to the greater good, the business becomes a force for positive change. This isn't about charity for show. It's about creating lasting value for your community, your employees, and your brand. When people see your business making a real effort to give back, they remember it. They talk about it. They want to work with you, support you, and stay loyal. That kind of reputation carries with you wherever you go. Build it well, and you can become the kind of leader others rally behind. Here are some practical ways to start weaving social responsibility into the fabric of your business:

Be inclusive.

Inclusivity is a foundational part of being a socially responsible business. When you commit to creating a space where everyone feels welcome, respected, and valued, you send a powerful message: This place is for everyone. Whether someone is a guest, employee, partner, or community member, they should never feel like they don't belong. Every interaction should communicate dignity, warmth, and openness. No one should feel overlooked, underestimated, or hesitant to engage with your staff or your space.

The truth is that every person who walks through your doors is part of your larger neighborhood. Treat them that way. When people see that your business genuinely values and embraces diversity, it enhances your brand's reputation, strengthens customer loyalty, and deepens community trust.

Help with a goal or purpose in mind.

While it's easy to write donation checks or hand out free passes in the name of goodwill, the most impactful contributions are those tied to a clear goal that benefits both your community and your business in a meaningful way. For example, if you operate a water park, consider offering free admission to families who are teaching their kids how to swim. Events like this promote safety, support families, and build positive associations with your brand. If you run a rock-climbing gym, you might host a community day focused on outdoor survival skills, giving people a valuable learning experience while introducing them to your facility. Whatever your initiative, make it personal and purposeful. Clearly communicate who you're helping, why it matters, and how it ties into your company's values. This not only deepens your impact but also builds trust and credibility. People are far more likely to support businesses that give back with a real sense of mission.

Consider giving time rather than money.

While financial donations are always appreciated, giving your time can be even more powerful. Time is our most limited resource, and when your team chooses to spend it serving others, people notice. It's easy to clock out after a forty-hour workweek and head straight home. That's why it means so much when businesses step up and volunteer their time for causes that matter. Whether it's joining a charity walk for JDRF or the American Cancer Society, helping out at a food bank, or mentoring local youth, showing up in person builds real relationships. It gives your business a human face and shows that you're part of the community.

Volunteering together also creates visibility in numbers. When people see you and your team out in the neighborhood actively supporting others, it builds trust and loyalty. They remember who showed up. And when it comes time to choose where to spend their money, they'll be far more likely to support the business that shows it cares.

Resist the temptation to toss money around freely.

As your business becomes known for its commitment to social responsibility, you'll likely receive more requests for donations. While that's a sign you're making a positive impact, it's also where strategy becomes essential. The truth is you can't support every cause, no matter how worthy. To remain profitable and sustainable, you need to be selective. Focus on partnerships and initiatives that align with your business values and make sense for your brand. Ask yourself, "Does this organization's mission reflect our purpose? Will this effort benefit both the community and the business in a meaningful way?"

Avoid the trap of giving reactively or out of guilt. Without a clear framework, leaders may start throwing money at causes that sound good on the surface but have no real connection to your goals or your guests. Your social responsibility strategy should be intentional, mission-driven, and grounded in long-term impact. By setting clear criteria for giving, you can ensure your contributions are thoughtful and truly effective.

When social responsibility becomes a core value, not just an occasional gesture, it leaves a lasting mark, ensuring your efforts will be remembered by the community for years to come. By showing up with purpose, contributing meaningfully, and aligning your values with real needs, your business can make a difference that outlives any single campaign. This is how you build a legacy that matters.

Key Takeaways

1. **Social responsibility builds lasting brand loyalty and community trust.**

   - When a business stands for something bigger than profit, it creates deep emotional connections with guests, team members, and the community.

   - Giving back generates goodwill, strengthens reputation, and makes the business memorable long after transactions end.

   - Purpose-driven actions increase team pride and motivation, especially among younger generations seeking value-aligned workplaces.

2. **A lack of social responsibility weakens relationships and reputation.**

   - Businesses that ignore community engagement lose opportunities for goodwill, visibility, and local support.

   - Poor relationships with community leaders can directly harm operations, such as by leading to blocked permits or licenses.

   - Without a sense of purpose beyond profit, companies struggle to inspire loyalty in guests or commitment in team members.

3. **Effective social responsibility is strategic, inclusive, and purpose-driven.**

   - Make inclusivity a core practice so everyone feels welcome and respected.

   - Focus contributions on initiatives that align with company values, have a clear mission, and benefit both the community and the business.

   - Prioritize meaningful engagement—whether through volunteering, partnerships, or targeted giving—over scattershot donations, ensuring long-term impact and sustainability.

Social Responsibility Self-Assessment Survey

Rate each question from 1 to 5.

(1 = Not true at all / 5 = Consistently true)

1. Does the business contribute meaningfully to the well-being of its community?

   Rating: ______

2. Are social responsibility efforts aligned with the company's mission and values?

   Rating: ______

3. Do leaders model respect, humility, and inclusivity in community interactions?

   Rating: ______

4. Does the business maintain ongoing relationships with community organizations?

   Rating: ______

5. Are contributions intentional and purpose-driven rather than reactive or guilt-based?

   Rating: ______

6. Do team members feel proud of how the organization gives back?

   Rating: ______

7. Do social initiatives strengthen trust and goodwill over time?

   Rating: ______

8. Is the business viewed as a positive presence in the community?

   Rating: ______

9. Are causes selected based on focus and impact rather than on volume?

   Rating: ______

10. Does leadership consider legacy—not just profit—when making decisions?

Rating: ______

Scoring & Interpretation

- **40–50 (Strong):** Purpose is embedded; the organization is trusted and remembered.

- **25–39 (Mixed):** Good intentions exist, but efforts lack consistency or focus.

- **10–24 (At Risk):** Disconnection from community is weakening trust and relevance.

Leader Reflection (Answer honestly!)

1. Would our community miss us if we closed tomorrow?
2. Are we giving back with intention—or only when asked?
3. Do our actions reflect who we claim to be?
4. Are we building long-term relationships or making one-time gestures?
5. What legacy would we leave behind today?

How to Use This Survey

- **Run annually during strategic planning.** Social responsibility should be intentional, not incidental.

- **Select focus areas.** Choose one to three causes aligned with your mission, community needs, and capacity.

- **Build relationships.** Prioritize partnerships over donations; long-term trust comes from consistency.

- **Engage the team.** Involve employees so responsibility becomes cultural pride, not leadership optics.

- **Measure impact.** Track participation, community feedback, partner engagement, and internal pride.

Conclusion
The Blueprint for Lasting Success

Excellence is not a singular act, but a habit. You are what you repeatedly do.

—Aristotle

When I started writing this book, my goal wasn't just to share stories from my career in turnarounds, growth strategies, and leadership. It was to give you a *blueprint*—a set of core values so practical, so battle-tested, that if you commit to them, they will fundamentally change your business, your team, and even your life.

Let's imagine for a moment that tomorrow you wake up and decide to *fully* apply the lessons from this book. What does that look like?

1. First, you lead with **integrity**. Your word is your bond. You do what you say you'll do—even when it's inconvenient. People trust you because your actions match your promises. This trust becomes the glue that holds everything together, especially in difficult times.

2. Then you layer in **accountability**. Every team member owns their results. No excuses, no finger-pointing. When mistakes happen, they're addressed quickly, with learning, not blame. Accountability turns intentions into measurable progress.

3. With **safety**, you minimize the risk of accidents and injuries so everyone at your business can relax and enjoy themselves. Your team learns to prioritize everyone's well-being and anticipate potential threats before they happen. This lowers your insurance rates and prevents bad press.

4. **Service** ensures that no matter how efficient your operations are, you never lose sight of the people you serve. You create moments worth remembering. Guests become advocates. Word of mouth spreads. Loyalty grows.

5. You strengthen that foundation with **communication**. Everyone knows the plan and the priorities as well as their role in achieving them. Problems don't get hidden; they get solved. Good communication eliminates confusion and builds alignment.

6. Through **commitment**, you and your team keep showing up—especially when it's hard. You stop seeing challenges as obstacles and start seeing them as opportunities to prove your resilience. This is the moment when a culture shifts from average to exceptional.

7. With **innovation**, you adapt and evolve. You listen, test, refine, and never settle. You make changes before the market forces you to. Innovation keeps you ahead of competitors and keeps your guests excited to come back.

8. Next comes **profitability**—your map to financial success. You paint a clear, compelling picture of how you plan to remain in the black. You adjust prices, portions, and other variables to ensure profits are consistently rising. This doesn't just inspire people; it focuses them.

9. **Partnership** extends your reach. You align with other organizations that share your values and goals. Together, you amplify each other's strengths, open new opportunities, and create value you couldn't have built alone.

10. Finally, **social responsibility** connects your work to something bigger than profit. You give back. You invest in your community. You make your business a source of pride, both for the people who work there and the people you serve.

11. If you've read this far, you know what happens when these values are absent. Without **integrity**, trust crumbles. Without

accountability, performance drops. Without **safety**, people get hurt. Without **service**, loyalty disappears. Without **communication**, confusion takes over. Without **commitment**, progress stalls. Without **innovation**, you fall behind. Without **profitability**, the company goes bankrupt. Without **partnership**, you stay isolated. Without **social responsibility**, your work lacks lasting meaning.

In short, without these values, you're vulnerable. With them, you're unstoppable.

Your Next Step

You don't have to overhaul everything at once. Start with one value. Introduce it, model it, and reinforce it until it becomes part of your culture. Then move to the next. The momentum will build naturally. Over time, these values will stop feeling like "initiatives" and start feeling simply like the way you do business.

Here's the challenge I'll leave you with:

1. Pick one value to focus on this month.
2. Commit to living it personally and visibly.
3. Teach it to your team members.
4. Hold yourself and others accountable to it.
5. Measure the impact.

Do this again with the next value. And the next. In a year, your business, your team, and maybe even your family will be unrecognizable—in the best way possible.

Parting Thoughts

I've seen businesses go from the brink of bankruptcy to record-breaking profits. I've seen locations with teams who once dreaded coming to work transform into high-energy, high-performance cultures. I've seen guests become loyal advocates for brands they love. And every single time, the turning point wasn't a miracle product, a lucky break, or a single superstar hire. It was a commitment to living out the values you've just learned in this book.

These values are the multiplier. They take whatever talent, resources, and opportunities you have and make them greater. They are the difference between being good and being truly great.

So my advice is simple: **Don't just read this book. Live it.** If you do, you won't just change your business. You'll change lives, starting with your own.

Tim Murphy
Founder and CEO, Murfeez Entertainment
CEO, TM Entertainment Consulting
Board Director, Coney Park and Happy City (Colombia, Peru, and Chile)
Former CEO, Boomers Parks (Boomers family entertainment centers and Big Kahuna's Water Parks)
Former CEO, Rebounderz Trampoline Parks (franchisor of trampoline parks)

Executive Self-Assessment Scorecard

Transfer the total score (10–50) from each chapter survey into the scorecard below.

Core Value	Score (10–50)	Status	Notes / Observations
Integrity	____ / 50	☐ Strong ☐ Mixed ☐ At Risk	__________ __________ __________
Accountability	____ / 50	☐ Strong ☐ Mixed ☐ At Risk	__________ __________ __________
Safety	____ / 50	☐ Strong ☐ Mixed ☐ At Risk	__________ __________ __________
Service	____ / 50	☐ Strong ☐ Mixed ☐ At Risk	__________ __________ __________
Communication	____ / 50	☐ Strong ☐ Mixed ☐ At Risk	__________ __________ __________

Core Value	Score (10–50)	Status	Notes / Observations
Commitment	____ / 50	☐ Strong ☐ Mixed ☐ At Risk	_______________ _______________ _______________
Innovation	____ / 50	☐ Strong ☐ Mixed ☐ At Risk	_______________ _______________ _______________
Profitability	____ / 50	☐ Strong ☐ Mixed ☐ At Risk	_______________ _______________ _______________
Partnership	____ / 50	☐ Strong ☐ Mixed ☐ At Risk	_______________ _______________ _______________
Social Responsibility	____ / 50	☐ Strong ☐ Mixed ☐ At Risk	_______________ _______________ _______________

Total System Score

Overall Score: _______ / 500

Big-Picture Interpretation

- **400–500 | High-Performance Organization:** Balanced, resilient, scalable. Protect strengths; close minor gaps.

- **250–399 | Inconsistent System:** Pockets of excellence exist; misalignment creates drag. Prioritize the lowest two categories.

- **Below 250 | Systemic Risk:** Culture or execution breakdown. Immediate leadership intervention required.

Areas of Imbalance

High scores in some areas do not compensate for failure in others. Use the patterns below as early warning indicators of systemic risk.

- **High Profitability + Low Integrity/Safety** → Short-term gains built on shortcuts, leading to trust erosion, incidents, or reputational damage.

- **High Service + Low Accountability** → Hard-working teams delivering inconsistent experiences, resulting in burnout and frustration.

- **High Innovation + Low Communication** → Constant change without clarity, creating confusion, resistance, and wasted effort.

- **High Commitment + Low Profitability** → Passionate teams pushing hard without sustainable economics, accelerating burnout.

- **High Accountability + Low Integrity** → Compliance without belief, where rules are followed only when enforced.

- **High Accountability + Low Service** → Efficient execution that feels cold and transactional and erodes guest loyalty.

- **High Safety (on paper) + Low Integrity** → False confidence masking hidden risks and underreported issues.

- **High Innovation + Low Accountability** → Ideas launched without follow-through, creating initiative fatigue.

- **High Social Responsibility + Low Accountability** → Good intentions without measurable impact, perceived as performative.

- **High Social Responsibility + Low Integrity/Communication** → Strong external reputation hiding internal distrust or confusion.

- **High Commitment + Low Communication** → High effort without alignment, resulting in motion without progress.

- **High Partnership + Low Profitability** → Positive relationships that dilute margins and strain sustainability.

- **High Profitability + Low Social Responsibility** → Financial success without purpose, weakening pride, retention, and long-term relevance.

Strengths become liabilities when they operate out of balance. Stabilize **integrity, safety, accountability,** and **communication** before amplifying performance or growth.

Executive Focus (Next 90 Days)

Select no more than three priorities:

Primary Priority: _______________________________

Secondary Priority: _______________________________

Stabilization Priority: _______________________________

Rule of thumb: You cannot scale what you cannot stabilize.